A PHILOSOPHY OF PAIN

A Philosophy of Pain

Arne Johan Vetlesen

Translated by John Irons

REAKTION BOOKS

Published by Reaktion Books Ltd
33 Great Sutton Street
London EC1V 0DX, UK

www.reaktionbooks.co.uk

This book was first published in 2004 by Dinamo Forlag
under the title *Smerte* by Arne Johan Vetlesen
©Arne Johan Vetlesen and Dinamo Forlag 2004

First published in English 2009
Reprinted 2010

English-language translation © Reaktion Books 2009
English translation by John Irons

Printed and bound in Great Britain
by CPI Antony Rowe, Chippenham, Wiltshire

British Library Cataloguing in Publication Data

Vetlesen, Arne Johan, 1960–
A philosophy of pain.
1. Pain—Philosophy.   2. Pain—Psychological aspects.
I. Title
128.4-dc22
ISBN: 978 1 86189 541 7

Contents

Introduction

Without pain our life is unthinkable. With it, life is hardly to be endured. When pain becomes total, it deprives us of life while still alive and causes us to long for the absence of pain – even though that would ultimately be synonymous with an end to life. If life is only a matter of pain, the question is whether it is worth living.

Living involves being exposed to pain every second – not necessarily as an insistent reality, but always as a possibility. The presence of pain varies from person to person. But the actual *exposure* to pain is something all human beings share – it is, quite simply, an essential part of the definition of the human condition.

The individual's relation to pain – to pain in his or her life – is one that cannot be exclusively determined by that individual. The society in which we live and the age to which we belong equip each one of us with a vocabulary and a yardstick for communicating about pain and assessing its significance. In terms of the body and the senses, pain is something we experience spontaneously, directly, in a non-circuitous way. The nature of our body and senses makes us susceptible to the sensation of pain, as we are to its opposites: pleasure and well-being.

Pain directly inflicted on the body reveals most clearly what pain *is*: pain is negative. I miss the block of wood with my axe and what I hit is my lower leg. I give a start, grimace, see the blood pour out of the cut – warm, dark, ominous. I scream. The sequence of events is so simple; everyone recognizes it: when pain is a stimulus, suffering is the response, understood as the protest made by the organism, a 'no' to what has been inflicted, since it is experienced as something that ought not to be, ought not to happen. The meaning of pain, if we can talk of such, is thus to be understood as *the inherent negativity of pain.* As a creature equipped with a body and senses, I cannot determine, cannot consider, whether pain is negative or not. No, to be affected by pain is synonymous with being affected by something negative, something undesirable. Pain presents itself as something which by its very nature is *against* me; therefore, my spontaneous response is to be *against* pain. Pain assumes the form of my enemy, the opposite of everything I desire for my own existence.

But is it that simple? Is pain unambiguous to that extent? Is there no room for interpretation, for evaluation – in short, for culture and communication?

There is, of course. That pain is to be considered as exclusively, by very definition negative – meaning that our relation to it consists of wishing it to disappear – is in itself the expression of a view that to a very high degree is historically and culturally determined. My assertion is that we, people living in one of the world's most affluent countries, have in the present age developed a conception of pain's position in human life that is possibly the most negative ever.

What do I mean by that? Do I wish to contest the fact that pain is something negative? That what is undesired grows out of pain itself, so to speak, rather than being something a particular culture has come up with?

The assertion I will seek to justify is not based on the idea that pain has been misunderstood when it is regarded as being something negative. The assertion is that this negative experience is not as obvious and not as spontaneous as we tend to believe. To be more precise, what is not obvious is that the negativity of pain is exclusively to be judged as negative. In short, that since something hurts, we are dealing with a type of experience that we ought to be without, and that we ought to do everything in our power to remove and prevent it.

For that is where we are, the culture we belong to in our part of the world. The most official confirmation of this really being so is, in my opinion, the World Health Organization's (who) definition of health as an optimum human state: by 'health' is meant the complete absence of pain and discomfort. The positivity of health is based on the (absolute) negativity of pain, so that the most ambitious goal for health is attained when pain, its enemy and opposite, is combated to such an extent that it is eliminated. We are dealing here with a declaration of war against pain 'and all its works', a declaration that is both supported and articulated by modern medical science. That Gro Harlem Brundtland, a qualified doctor and with a past as a social-democratic prime minister in 'the best country in the world' to live in, was the leader of the who when this definition of health was announced, is in every way apposite.

Such a conception of health, one that includes the wish for pain to be eliminated, does not only say something about the who. It also says a great deal about the prevalent view in our present-day society. If by 'pain' we are referring to everything that hurts, and consider everything that hurts to be undesirable, it seems logical to concentrate all our resources and our knowledge on winning the human fight against pain. And it seems as if a goal that in earlier and more primitive ages must have appeared to be totally unrealistic, inconceivable even, can now be reached – especially thanks to advances in medical science and the technologies it utilizes in its fight against all kinds of disease.

Why should there be anything wrong with such a goal? Will not all of us, given our common exposure to pain, torment and suffering, unanimously and unhesitatingly back such an aim? Is it possible to hold the opposite view and be entitled to be believed and be in one's right mind? What would such an opposite view be based on: that pain is good, that it contains something inherently desirable? In this book I am prepared to be a spokesman for such an opposite view, though with important qualifications, as we shall see. Let us take an initial look at what the point of view represents.

A first step on the way to demonstrating a view of pain that refuses to accept that it is exclusively negative in human life and that it ought to be removed as far as is practically possible is to ask the question: Is it really true that we only experience pain as being negative and unwanted? The axe-blow to the leg *is* painful, it *does* hurt, and all I want then and there is for the pain to stop. So the experience of pain is one that is negative through and through. Have I not thereby also answered the question as to whether pain can appear to be anything else that negative and unwanted? Have I not, with the aid of a completely unambiguous example, shown that it cannot – not for any normal human being exposed to pain who is still in possession of his faculties? Why want anything that is painful?

That human beings naturally, and without needing to consider it, strive for what they regard as good, or what seems to promise pleasure (not least bodily and sensual pleasure), is a claim on which all of moral philosophy rests, although admittedly in such differing variants as the ethics of virtue à la Aristotle and utilitarianism (the ethics of utility) à la Jeremy Bentham. The connection can be expressed most directly by saying that something is good *because* we connect it with pleasure. Thus we have a natural disposition for seeking the good – that which from a moral point of view is felt to be worth striving for since it will be identical with – or at least part of – what we as corporeal-sensual beings are disposed to do. The task of morality is to create a recognition of the fact that all people have a *right* to seek to maximize the experience (utilitarian: amount) of pleasure by means of their acts, but that everyone must at the same time respect the principle of not seeking personal pleasure in a way that will hinder the right of others to do the same. Admittedly, there can be differing conceptions of how this can best be achieved and guaranteed in a way that is good for everyone. But the fact that everyone, presumably spontaneously and without stopping to consider, is prepared to agree with this understanding as the perfectly natural point of departure for every form of ethics and every plan for developing a good society can hardly be doubted, if at all. Or can it? As I intend to show later, strong arguments can be advanced against this point of departure, including ethical ones. Let me, however, begin the problematization elsewhere.

That we as human beings detest and fear pain is not some invention of the modern father of utilitarianism, Jeremy Bentham. Even if this were to be true – of all human beings and all known societies – it is far from being the whole story. For while it is true that we shun pain, it is equally true that it turns us on, it excites us and that we actively seek it. In short, pain is not something neutral: we are not indifferent to it, and those instances where we actually are seem striking and call for an explanation. In line with what I have said above, pain, then, is *charged*. What we need to realize is that the chargedness of pain is not synonymous with its negativity. It is quite common to experience something fascinating, attractive and in that sense positive about pain or the prospect of pain. That this is so is not excluded by the fact that a moral assessment will usually consider pain as being negative, as something that ought not to exist and should therefore be relieved or eased to the extent it is encountered. Our moral propensity to condemn and banish pain, to pursue every person who deliberately inflicts (unnecessary and unwanted) pain on others, thus contrasts completely with our (from a psychological point of view) quite normal propensity to be fascinated by pain, in recognition of the fact that there is more to pain that its alleged negativity.

To see where this leads us we need to delve deeper into the phenomenon itself, deeper than both the oversimplified moral understanding and the common-sense psychology that we have used so far. And it is certainly necessary to ask some fundamental questions that have not yet been raised. One such question is: is pain something unavoidable? or, more precisely: by 'pain' are we talking about a phenomenon that unavoidably is, and always will be, present in the life of every individual? A second, just as basic question is: is pain as uniform a phenomenon as we have provisionally assumed? Is the pain released when I hit my leg with an axe an adequate image of what pain is, or how pain behaves and what it means in human existence?

Once these questions have been asked, it strikes us that so far we have tacitly allowed physical, externally inflicted pain to be the model for what pain is and what reactions it causes. There are many reasons for a description of the phenomenon of pain beginning with physical pain: it is visible (observable), not only to the person involved but also to others; its cause and effects are in principle possible to ascertain and possible to intervene in medically, although the prospect of relieving and curing will depend on the degree of seriousness as well as the medical action available. The pain we are dealing with here is an *injury*. As such it is contingent, i.e. something that occurred, that has the nature of a particular event (the blow of the axe), an event that, however, can be considered as avoidable: the injury resulted from an accident. We can examine the example from other angles to reveal other aspects. If you strike me on the leg with an axe, the assessment of this event will depend on whether the pain inflicted on me in this instance was due to your striking me deliberately or inadvertently. In the former case the fact that the infliction of pain was deliberate will give rise to moral indignation, maybe even a punitive reaction. In the latter case the moral condemnation will not materialize or will be milder. And, finally, if I am considered to have intentionally injured myself, the initial reaction will be psychological rather than moral, in the form of wonder: why on earth did you hit yourself on the leg with an axe? That someone intentionally harms another person is something we know constantly happens; it is something we learn within our culture to detest and condemn; however, it is not something that necessarily rouses our wonder. Motives for doing something like that can be many, and the stuff of which they are made will be familiar to most of us, since we cannot, hand on heart, claim never to have wished to inflict pain on somebody else. To decide to inflict strong physical pain on oneself where it could have been completely avoided is, however, something of a mystery in many cases. It is an act that raises questions of whether the person in question is of a completely sound mind, of whether he knows what he is doing, about his reasons for doing it. Intentional serious physical self-injury is a psychological challenge rather than a moral one, a task for therapy rather than for the guardians of morality and punitive institutions. It is instructive to examine why this is so – something I intend to do below.

Physical pain – inflicted by others or by oneself – is, in other words, not synonymous with pain as such, even though we feel it is perfectly natural to take it as our point of departure for an understanding of what pain is. If we do so, we are in a sense starting *from the outside*. We are adopting a visual perspective, we are observers, and we can observe other people's pain, just as we can observe our own. As stated, the cause – what it is that triggers the pain – is normally easy to determine, as are the effects. If the pain is serious, it is a task for medicine to alleviate; pain makes us sufferers, the type of sufferers who become patients and who require the help of doctors to have it relieved. Relief here is what could be called the human response and intervention that pain regularly asks for: the inherent aim of physical pain is the cessation of pain. Anyone afflicted by this pain, in this way, will experience it in the same way, will desire the cessation of the pain, in a kind of universal human state, where all other differences between those afflicted with pain (the sufferers) that are otherwise real cease to have any meaning. Two soldiers who are fighting against each other and who define each other on the basis of mutual and reciprocal enmity will naturally expect the same reaction to physical pain in the other person as in himself.

True enough, we can feel ourselves all alone in our intense physically inflicted pain, especially in situations where no one around us has, or has had, a corresponding pain. My pain is my loneliness; it strengthens and clarifies the feeling I have of being alone in the world, alone with and in my body, which separates me physically from everything else in the world. The mineness of the body is identical with the mineness of the pain: both are now in a radical – or unknown and unsensed – sense 'mine only', not other people's. Pain forces me backwards, or downwards; it forces me back to a purely physical-biological level, stripped of all abilities, dispositions and dimensions of my human existence that are over and above – precisely *over and above* – elementary physical existence.

Let us pause for a while and consider two states of intense pain, the one extreme and relatively rare, the other all too common – torture and serious illness.

ONE

Pain in Extremis: Torture

Torture is man's most refined method for forcing a person to an utter, total abandonment of – or withdrawal from – everything that normally constitutes the extra-physical in existence. Torture is to bring the person to the point where the specifically human qualities of existence are abandoned, where they are eliminated, and in a way that the person can do nothing but helplessly register, unable to prevent or reverse this process. The person enters torture as a human being and is dragged out as an animal, still alive when considered as a body, but lifeless as a human subject. Every blow, every jolt, every shock of pain inflicted on the body aims at speeding up this transformation from human to merely animal existence.

Torture is considered an extreme form of inflicting pain, but precisely for that reason it sheds light on aspects of pain that lie concealed in our everyday lives. In her pioneer study *The Body in Pain*, American scholar Elaine Scarry begins by pointing out that physical pain is unique among all our mental, somatic and sensuous states by virtue of the fact that such pain does not have any object: physical pain is an intentional state (it is about something, not blind), but what pain is 'about', that which gives it its content, does not have the form of an object, something it is possible to refer to in the world. Even though the ability to experience physical pain is a just as elementary, indeed primitive, fact of being a human being as is the ability to hear, to touch, to desire, to fear, to be hungry, it differs from all of these and from all other physical and mental characteristics by not pointing towards an object in the outside world. While the basic senses – hearing, sight, taste, touch, smell – take us out of ourselves, out towards particular objects in the outside world, pain is not 'about' something or 'for' something. We say: 'it's painful', possibly 'it hurts'. But what is 'it'? Shouldn't we rather say 'I hurt', or 'the hurt is me'? Language, with its tendency to link everything that is to be communicated to particular referents, falls sadly short. And that is because pain as such is object-less. At this elementary level the object-less is also the language-less. We thus express pain by regressing in terms of language, by turning to sounds that are reminiscent of our animal existence, sounds that originally come from a repertoire that precedes socially learned verbal language.

According to Scarry's analysis, physical pain is what above all other states marks an absolute division between persons, between you and me. To be in pain is to have absolute certainty; my pain contains an indubitability I do not know from any other context. My physical pain cannot be taken away from me; since it has a bodily location, I cannot flee from it, even though it is well known – not least from literary representations – that people in extreme pain try to flee from their own bodies, out of their bodies, to escape the pain. Contrasting with the indubitability and unremovability of my pain, we have the dubitability of the other person's pain. The one who has the pain will without any effort grasp it, be filled by it; the one who does not have the pain will without any effort *not* grasp it, not be filled by it. To see other people's pain, to hear about other people's pain is, according to Scarry, like a model of what we believe can be doubted. From this derives pain's dual nature, according to whether it is mine or someone else's: pain is in existence as that which absolutely cannot be doubted and that absolutely can be doubted.

In Scarry's terminology pain is not an emotion (for emotions take objects, as fear towards the danger I am confronting)

16

but a state. Pain resists language, as we have seen, since it is unsuitable for the kind of objectivization on which language depends. Absolute or total pain involves the annihilation of language; from a political perspective, the targeted infliction of pain on particular victims is a method of annihilating their language, their language as their specific cultural way of being in the world, of having, talking about and interpreting a world. (Scarry talks in this sense about how the self of the victim as well as his *voice* is sought to be annihilated, 'voice' understood as an individual's ability to articulate mental content and thus communicate his 'world' to others.) So pain, as the pain in the person who experiences it, is 'inexpressible'. It is significant that we, as we fumble in our attempts to find words for pain, use phrases like 'it is as if . . .' or 'it feels now as if . . .' without ever precisely being able to grasp this thing that pain is similar to. We have an urge to make something that can be communicated and shared out of what above everything else in our lives is originally internal and not capable of being shared.

The nature of torture is stable to a rare degree. Its distinct forms and methods are repeated everywhere, from age to age and culture to culture, with only small variations on the same basic elements. Torture consists of two acts: the mainly physical act, the infliction of pain, and the mainly verbal act, the interrogation, asking the victim questions. The first act seldom takes place without the second. How is the relationship between the two to be understood?

Scarry maintains that the relationship is often misunderstood. It is misunderstood because the way in which the aim of torture is presented by the torturers – or the political powers behind them – is so easily accepted as the gospel truth, i.e. that the pain inflicted is the means to an end, in the form of the information divulged at the interrogation. But this is turning things upside-down. The pain *is* the end, not the means to something else; the reference to informa-

interrogation as a form of pain / torture

tion is nothing else than a pretended motive of the torturers, one that gives pain a purely instrumental function and that, logically assessed, opens up the possibility of obtaining the information it refers to *without* the use of pain – which is precisely what is not practised. In the interrogation, the torturer asks the victim questions *as if* the as yet unanswered questions are what motivates the cruelty, *as if* the answers to them are what is absolutely crucial. But the fact that questions are asked as if the answers mean something does not prove that they mean anything at all. So what is the real purpose of the interrogation, of all the questions? If the answers that are finally extorted do not have the importance they are claimed to have, why could you not just as well drop the interrogation and exclusively inflict pain?

The answer Scarry gives is that the interrogation – the fact that one party asks questions and the other has to answer – gives the torture a psychological-motivational basis and a moral justification, or, more correctly, gives the appearance of this. The point is that when the interrogation is carried out, 'confessions' will often follow, and such confessions – where other persons are often betrayed, sometimes including those closest to the victim (spouse, child, friends, political allies) – have the status of a breach of faith, the seriousness of which depends on who is being betrayed, and what the betrayal might mean for their subsequent fate. To talk of a breach of faith, confession and betrayal, to talk of those who crack up and those who manage to resist, those who crack up easily or quickly and those who never do so, no matter the trials and tribulations – this is to talk in a non-neutral, i.e. morally charged language.

This brings us closer to the more profound point, the one that answers the question why torture contains interrogation. For what happens is that the victim of torture is ascribed a moral responsibility, a kind of agency: the victim is a person who offers resistance or who betrays, one who is strong or one who is weak, one who can put up with much pain or one who can put up with little, one who unselfishly puts up with the greatest stress so that others may go free, or one who succumbs when the pain is felt and the fear of one's own skin and own welfare overshadows everything else. In short, as outsiders and as societies we all participate in this kind of morally charged use of language towards, and assessment of, the victim, of the individual victim's 'efforts' or 'performance' under what we – without realizing the seriousness of it – refer to as 'inhuman conditions'. The answer to the question we asked is therefore that the function of the interrogation in general and the confession in particular is to block the otherwise spontaneous preoccupation with the victim's actual pain, in the form of possible sympathy or pity. By presenting torture as a somewhat 'random' method for achieving a goal that is supposed to be external to torture in the form of information/confession/betrayal, attention is shifted – that of everyone, the torturer and the victim no less that the outsider – *away* from the infliction of pain to which the victim is subjected, and thereby away from the victim as a person who arouses sympathy. Attention is diverted instead to the victim as the centre of the entire process, though not *as* victim but as a player (himself responsible), as the party whose actions – to speak or remain silent – determine the degree of pain that is inflicted. Being a player and an important element in the ascribing of moral responsibility are thus diverted from the torturer to his victim – just as the torturer wants. In short, it is the victim's so-called 'active' contribution in determining his own fate that is placed centre stage.

When the victim confesses as a result of the infliction of pain during torture, outsiders tend to describe this as abandoning everything that until then has been important for him: family, friends, fatherland, the cause and the ideal he has fought for, been willing to sacrifice his life for should it be necessary. Everything that the self is composed of in a psychological sense is betrayed and renounced. For the torture victim himself, however, things are different. For what the infliction of pain achieves is that this created world, with all its psychological and mental content, everything that language normally objectifies, communicates and maintains, this entire created world outside the body ceases to feel real, to feel valid. The only real and valid thing – reality pure and simple – is now turned in on the subject himself instead of outwards towards a common world. All that is real is the body. The body consists of pain, the body is pain and pain is the body. Everything else is non-existent, non-important, lightness itself. The pain is intensified until it mimics death, where all sensations point towards death as the real, and away from life. Since death is now something 'imminent', or can occur 'at any moment', it has already begun.

Pain and power are the two absolutely incompatible entities in torture. They are inversely proportional to each other: the greater the victim's pain, the greater is the power of the torturer. The presence of pain means the loss of a world, the familiar world of mental content, of initiative and meaning; the absence of pain means the presence of a world. To the same extent as the torturer increases the victim's physical pain – the pain that causes him to lose his world – the torturer increases his power to define that world completely. What happens in torture is that a person's physical pain is transformed into and is perceived as another person's power. While, as we have seen, it is usual to ascribe the torturer a motive, and thereby a particular mental content, namely to extort so-called 'valuable information', the confession of the victim, the fact that at a certain point he 'cracks up' and starts to talk, is such that he abandons all his mental content, that he forgoes his specific mental world. What ostensibly means everything for the torturer finally means nothing for the victim.

This touches on a general condition of strong physical pain. Only when the body is taken care of, when its functions are intact and the body operates within secure surroundings, can consciousness interact with all the senses and address the outside world; only then can the person have a world full of mental content. This outward orientation, which is so crucial for human intentionality and agency – and so taken for granted by all of us in our normal everyday lives – is radically undermined in the event of torture in particular and of intense physical pain in general. Pain causes the body to turn in towards the person; more precisely, the bodily functions are twisted – the ability to move, hunger, thirst, defecation, the sensory apparatus – outwards, in a perverse enlargement, distortion and transformation of their distinctive nature under normal conditions. The trick of the torturer is to make the victim's body his worst enemy: to turn the victim's body into the most effective tool in the infliction of pain, in the absolutization of the person *as* a body quite simply, and thereby in the loss – the annihilation – of the person's world, of his ability to 'have' a world outside himself, outside the body. The body becomes absolutely present *because* it is being annihilated, because the annihilation of it is so painful that the pain forces the person to abandon all other mental content, all other objects of his attention and sensory ability. Torture demonstrates that physical pain possesses the power to annihilate a person's world, self and voice.

In normal instances a person's pain will be subjectively real but non-objectivized and invisible to everyone else. In torture a solid objectification of the pain is undertaken, since it is turned outwards and becomes visible to everyone who can see – an indubitable reality in a common outside world – only to be denied at the same instant. For that is precisely what happens, according to Scarry's analysis. The 'world' that is formed by those observing the pain, first and foremost by those directly inflicting it, who have the power to increase and decrease the pain in the victim and stop only to begin once more, is a world of observers who see the pain in the victim only to deny its (mental-human and moral) real nature. This is where we glimpse the structure of torture: first the infliction of physical pain, then the objectification (the visible manifestation) of the subjective attributes of pain (the screams, the blood, the spasmodic jerking, the twisted limbs) and, finally, the translation or transformation of pain's objectivizing attributes to the insignia of power, to a demonstration of the omnipotence of the torturers and the regime they represent – an omnipotence that functions as a parasite on (a direct function of) the powerlessness in the form of abandonment of self, world and voice that is extorted from the victim and that has the 'confession' as its preferred form of proof. In short, the outwardly turned, now visible repertoire of inflicted and inflictable pain is interpreted *as if* it is a demonstration of the power of the torturer and the regime. The more massive the former, the more increased the latter.

What can make the torturer stop? That the reality of the other person's pain enters the consciousness of the torturer (Scarry) or, to put it my way, that the torturer opens himself to being emotionally affected by the victim's affectedness. That this does *not* take place is, of course, not coincidental. It is the very condition for torture being able to take place and to continue, no matter how annihilated the victim gradually becomes as a result of the pain. Inflicting pain and objectivizing pain have the denial of the human reality of pain as both cause and effect in a self-increasing spiral: the denial is the act on the part of the torturer that is increased by what he does and that increases what he does as he continues. What happens is not that the power experienced by the torturer makes him blind, or that his power presupposes his blindness; the relationship is instead quite simple: 'his blindness, his willed amorality, *is* his power, or at least a large part of it'.[1]

The relationship of all known civilizations to the human body consists in the body being transcended in ways that are reconcilable with, indeed, that guarantee the body's basic needs: by building a house, by providing warmth, by procuring and preparing food, by ensuring toilet facilities, etc. Cultural arrangements and rituals contribute to the body being taken care of in an adequate manner, with the result that human consciousness in all its functions can turn outwards towards the world, in going beyond the body in a way that has, then, the intactness of the body as its vital – and usually unspoken – prerequisite. Torture can be defined as a reversal of this civilizing element. As we know from documented cases of torture throughout the world – most recently from the much-discussed Abu Ghraib prison run by the Americans in Iraq – the victim is exposed to the absolute shock involved in being a witness to – indeed, quite literally being the subject of – the various normally body-caring cultural artefacts and rituals being transformed one by one from a caring and body-transcending function into the exact opposite, i.e. into a weapon in the annihilation of the body's intactness and capacity to turn its attention to the world outside it.

How does this take place? Concretely, by the torturer, as one of the first things he does when the victim is led in, acting as a guide in the surroundings where the torture is about to start: 'Look,' he says, picking up certain kitchen utensils the victim is familiar with from their everyday use, 'here we have a sharp carving knife, here you can see an empty glass bottle; over there are a table and a chair. We are going to find plenty of uses now for all of these things.' In other words, everything that prior to the torture is part of the protection and security offered by the physical outside world, everything that used to help protect the body and satisfy its needs, is now ruthlessly turned against it in the form of a number of implements designed to annihilate the body, with its needs and functions now changed – turned inside out – so as to turn them into so many means for the intensification of pain. That which used to be synonymous with pleasure and enjoyment – eating, drinking, the sexual organs – are methodically changed into embodied possibilities (scenarios) for the infliction of extreme displeasure and humiliation. Scarry describes this transformation as a zero sum game between the elements pain and power, the physical and the mental, divided into the roles of torturer and prisoner.

> Although the torturer dominates the prisoner both in physical acts and in verbal acts, ultimate domination requires that the prisoner's ground become increasingly physical and the torturer's increasingly verbal, that the prisoner become a colossal body with no voice [to articulate a world with, a mental content] and the torturer a colossal voice [a voice composed of two voices, his own and the extorted one of the other person, in the form of a confession or a cracking up] with no body, that eventually the prisoner experiences himself exclusively in terms of sentience and the torturer in terms of self-extension. All those ways in which the torturer dramatizes his opposition to and distance from the prisoner are ways of dramatizing his distance from the body. The most radical act of distancing resides in his disclaiming of the other's hurt.[2]

It is no exaggeration to claim that the denial by the torturer of the other person's pain is the main prerequisite on which successful torture is based. The moment a torturer lets go of such a denial, with the result that he begins to feel emotionally affected by what he is actually carrying out – the wholesale destruction of another human being (speaking metaphorically: reaching from what is bodily external to what is mentally most internal) – it will (possibly) mark the end of his career as a proficient torturer. For what a torturer needs to keep insisting on is that the pain that so blatantly obviously is being inflicted upon and so utterly pains the victim has only a physical reality as opposed to a moral reality of the kind that involves co-human identification and being emotionally affected. The proficient torturer is a person with a sharply objectivizing insight into the victim's weak spots, for precisely what it is that causes most pain, and as such is most efficient in crushing the person and his or her entire world. In order to hold onto this insight, to cultivate it in its one-dimensionality, the torturer has to deny and neutralize every tendency to feel or empathize with the victim, rather than just coolly observe him and in a detached manner register the reactions caused by the infliction of pain. The objectification involved here presents the victim as an *it*; letting go of the objectification will involve allowing the victim to step forward as a *you*. The ideologically conditioned changing of another person into 'one of *them*', into a representative – interchangeable as such – of a hated or feared or despised group in an us-versus-them scheme, can only be neutralized when these collective and distancing modes of description are replaced by the spontaneous and emotionally based meeting between two human individuals: a meeting where both are first and foremost themselves, not embodiments or reminders of collective entities one has been taught to fear, to combat, with the other always as 'one of them', i.e. one of the Jews, one of the communists, one of the capitalists, one of the terrorists. To allow the other person to step forward as an individual, with his individuality in the foreground, means to allow the meeting with him (or her) – the torturer's victim – to assume a human and moral quality, which will mean that the torturer for his part feels his individual responsibility for what he now *chooses* to do to his victim.

TWO

Lasting Pain: Illness

Torture is a drastic example, experienced by few. People with a particularly painful illness (especially of a chronic nature) can, however, experience something similar, in the sense that life is reduced to pain, and that a life that only 'is' pain, restless and hopeless pain, involves a completely different form of existence than that previously known – and taken for granted – by the healthy person. It is said that people with chronic (incurable) syphilis, especially the neurosyphilis variant (where all control of bodily functions ceases so that all movements take the form of violent spasms) are those who have the most radical experience of the total transformation of this life into pain. The pain experience places everything else at a lower level, allows no space, no second to recur outside itself, untouched and intact. The total state of pain is thus identical with the total emptying of meaning, of desire. A person deprived of desire, for whom nothing in life no longer has any meaning or purpose, is no longer a person in the sense of a seat of human subjectivity. But what about the pain that is not physical? The pain that is invisible, that is not inflicted from without?

Man's exposure to pain is not first and foremost an exposure to physical pain. When the axe strikes the leg, I am injured; the injury has its own objectivity, it can be observed by others and those with a suitable competence can seek to heal it. I presume that the pain released by the axe-blow against my leg will be precisely the same and thus behave in the same way and result in the same reaction and need for alleviation for anyone exposed to the same. Simply as human beings we assume that we are fundamentally similar as regards exposure and reaction to such pain inflicted from the outside. The differences between us as individuals have no role to play. As regards the sensation of physical pain, we believe that we are transparent to each other, eminently understandable, across cultures and historical epochs. Nevertheless, we know – only too well – that this comprehensibility can be blocked, that it can be put out of action and replaced by an experience of absolute distance and non-identification concerning *others'* pain, while the suffering sensation of one's own pain persists. While Elaine Scarry, as we have seen, postulates such an absolute difference – indeed, abyss – between *my* pain and *your* pain as an 'ontological division', I would conversely claim that visible physical pain in someone else spontaneously seems to be something understandable to me, something I recognize because of my own experience and that I now naturally ascribe to the other person who seems to be experiencing 'the same'. The division Scarry postulates as being original and ontological is not so in my opinion, rather something that calls for an explanation, something that is produced and becomes dominant under special conditions. That such conditions are real in many situations and that they are continually being re-created is something I accept beyond a doubt, which gives Scarry's above analysis its empirical topicality.

Why do we believe that our physical exposure to pain is understandable, or even transparent, for each other, as I claim? Is it because the physical pain directs attention to what has to do with the body, and that we consider the corporeal as being what, above everything else, we share with everyone else? This is how medicine and science view humans as corporeal beings and it is also a common-sense view of the body. In terms of both its functions and its exposure to pain the body is *one*, in the sense that it is the same for all individuals – although with certain variations based on gender and age, though not so great that any woman cannot get to know her body by reading the book *Woman, Know Your Body* – a book for all is precisely what the topic 'body' allows. Only by assuming that the body is identical in all individuals (of the same gender) can the professions that specialize in the needs of the body – its illness, its ageing process, etc. – use their knowledge of the average human body on all the individual examples of it that they actually have to subject to treatment.

So the body's specific and physiological homogeneity provides a scientific basis for the general conception that physical pain is something that behaves in a fundamentally similar way for all humans exposed to it. To put it another way: it is my body as a human body that determines what causes pain, not me as a unique individual and as a bearer of my own body. True enough, the body that shudders with pain as a result of the slash wound inflicted on me is *my* body, no one else's; I experience my body's pain in the first person singular, and I may well doubt your expressed assurance that you know and not least *feel* 'exactly what I am going through'. In my physically inflicted pain I therefore experience myself as anything but interchangeable. To the extent that the experience of pain changes anything at all in my relationship to the outside world in general and other people in particular, the change consists in my being cast out into a kind of *aloneness* I had not experienced before pain invaded my life. The more total, the more all-pervasive the pain becomes, the more the presence and possible variations in depth, intensity and length of the pain assume the nature of being the sole theme in my existence, the more strongly I can experience it as a withdrawal from a common human universe of which I was a member prior to the pain striking, on an equal footing with everybody else. When it is only pain and me everything is all about, it is as if I cannot manage to tear myself away from myself, myself reduced to a body, and thereby to what philosophers call *pure immanence*: the body as a prison, with its physical-spatial extent, and thus limits, as being one with the limits of my world. Since pain throws me back on myself, myself as a body and *only a body*; since the body is scarcely capable of bearing me, of supporting my mere physical-biological existence, I hardly have the strength to cope with my body and thereby my own existence any longer. I am reaching the point where I hardly have the strength to live, since life has ceased to be stretched out between pleasure and discomfort, joy and fear, spark and extinction. The alternation between what causes me to feel good and what causes me pain has ceased to exist – only one of the dimensions is still valid.

In other words, I maintain that physical pain understood as exposure to pain has something universally human about it, something we can share an experience of. But as soon as we start to dwell on what such pain does to me, especially when it is particularly intense or long-lasting (perhaps chronic), a strongly individualizing element enters. I am exposed to something all human beings can be exposed to, in principle. But it is *my* way of tackling this state that we are dealing with here – and precisely this can be experienced as radically separating me from all other human beings.

The taking over of my life and my vitality by bodily pain does not only threaten to isolate me, cause me to feel alone in relation to everything around me. It does not only threaten to restrict the entire world to one single point: pain's non-dislodgable reality, that turns the world into a place for pain and nothing else, that makes my pain my world. For when pain, now exclusively a seat of all that causes pain, restricts my existence in the world, I lose the experience of being of equal value with and fully intelligible to other people. From now on it is, on the one hand, me and my pain, and on the other, all the rest, those without pain. The more I merge with

Own pain is experienced very differently from someone else's pain, even if its attribution is experienced. Every human being experiences their experienced pain.

my body as a sufferer, the more I slide away from other people and all their projects that *transcend* the body and pain out there in the great big world.

Did we not, though, speak earlier of a species-specific solidarity and an eminent transparency and intelligibility based on the basic similarity of all human bodies – a similarity in everything essential, a dissimilarity in everything unessential? Are we unable now, gazing with the eye of a sufferer at the world, to see that if the body takes up all of existence, nothing would seem to be more threatened, more unattainable, than precisely such a self-evident, all-inclusive solidarity and intelligibility? Is it not so that the person whose existence is essentially nothing but suffering experiences himself as different, as not being understood by others (those fit and healthy), as one who is almost ostracized?

The insight that crowds in is that the body – the body's exposure to pain – can just as well be claimed to be something that divides people as something that unites us all. It is the pain that decides: the pain determines whether I experience myself and my existence in the world as fundamentally equal with, and a part of, the existence of other people in it, or whether I conversely experience my existence as radically disconnected from that of others. So there is no point in giving an unequivocal answer based on the body as such; the pain that takes over, dominates, annihilates the body makes a considerable difference, determining whether my experienced equality and equal value with everyone else as human beings is simply replaced by a demarcating isolation from what is universally human. Anyone who has experienced this is well aware of the difference.

The message of this analysis, in other words, is that physical pain, because it is bound to the body, *individualizes* – indeed, that such bodily pain individualizes more the stronger the sensation of pain is, i.e. the more strongly its presence stamps the person's being-in-the-world, experience of himself and everything else in the world. The ability of physical pain to individualize, in the sense of *mark the difference*, between the sufferer and everyone else, is often overlooked. As I have pointed out, the medical-scientific view and the common-sense view of physical pain have opposite messages: that since such pain is something everyone as bodily beings are exposed to and what is more, exposed to in a similar way, such pain is one of the phenomena that connect and unite all human beings, by virtue of the exposure to pain as something we all have.

The overriding difference – one that creates so many others – is between exposure to pain as a universally human potential and as an experienced reality: the latter is always bound to the individual and therefore dependent on the person. We live our lives as beings exposed to pain. That applies to all of us. The exposure is something we have in common. But the pain that strikes always strikes in the form of a particular event in a particular person's life.

Where has this brought us? Is the point I wish to arrive at the well-known one that 'it's not how you feel but *what you make* of how you feel'? That the same type of pain infliction gives rise to different reactions in different people? That as soon pain shifts from a universally human potential to a concrete here-and-now reality for *me*, but not for you, there is a shift from the similar to the dissimilar? That how I deal with my pain even says in a special way something profound and essential about who I am, i.e. a pain-transmitted exposure and clarification of my individuality, my differing nature? In short, am I making an assertion about pain as *principium individuationis*?

To answer such questions we need to broaden the perspective on what pain actually is and what forms it can take.

THREE

Psychic Pain

The perspective I have adopted so far must be broadened in highly dissimilar directions. First, I will shift the focus away from pain as something physical, inflicted from the outside, to pain as something mental. Later, the perspective on pain will change from seeing pain as something we detest and fear to something we are fascinated and attracted by, so as to do full justice to the Janus face of pain.

What is psychic pain? Can such pain display characteristics that correspond to the visibility of physical pain? Is the objectivity that traditionally applies to physical pain replaced in the case of psychic pain by something completely subjective? Can we make any general statements about what psychic pain is and (not least) what forms it takes for the individual, as we are used to doing with physical pain?

As mentioned, from both a common-sense and medical-science point of view, physical pain is considered to be the most indubitable and 'objective' form of pain. Psychic pain, on the other hand, is something second-rate, or secondary and derived – a phenomenon with a weight of explanation that physical pain is exempt from as a matter of course. When the doctor has not found obvious 'physical' causes of the patient's pain, the general view has been that the patient is not in any pain, or alternatively that 'it's only mental', i.e. it is not something that is real, rather something the patient is simulating.

This is – yet again – an indication that the classical division between physical and psychic pain does more harm than good, as regards both understanding and treatment. We also see the problem in an opposite variant, namely when psychiatric patients complain of bodily pains and psychiatric staff say that the patient is 'somatizing' his afflictions. We can see that both traditions of treatment – somatics and psychiatry – have a selective approach to what pain is: pain is either something physical, *or* it is something mental. In concrete situations this creates the well-known problem that the patient risks not being believed in his attempts to communicate his subjective experience of pain to the staff.[3] Having said that, I would add that in present-day treatment practice we relatively seldom meet unadulterated versions of the one or the other conception of pain.

Let us for the time being hold on to the idea that pain – as I intend to understand it from now on – always has both a physical and a mental (psychological) component; these two main components 'compose' the concrete experience of pain, which, viewed thus, is a complex phenomenon. In the simplest sense pain is physical in that it is experienced in the body as 'I am in pain'. The point is that this applies – though less obviously – to psychic pain as well, i.e. not only for such experiences as the pain felt at the blow of an axe. Grief or experiences of loss, major defeats or powerful fear are all examples of a pain with a mental origin, but that nevertheless can find expression in diffuse stomach pains, headache, nausea, dizziness, stiffness, etc. Sorrow is certainly a form of mental suffering – just think of the English word 'heartbreak', for example. Heavy, long-lasting sorrow, however, is always something physical in the ways mentioned. As we shall gradually clearly see, it is this complexity of the corporeal-somatic and the psychological-mental that in my analysis I include in the phenomenon of pain.

I would like to start my account of psychic pain by referring to the insight into such pain that, in my opinion, is offered by psychoanalysis, in preference to all competing approaches. By making this detour to psychoanalytic thinking about pain we can also place classical medicine's understanding of pain in critical relief. And that is important, since medicine has strongly influenced – we could say 'made scientific' – the general conception of what pain is in the modern age. The fact that the psychoanalytic approach has been controversial in our culture ever since Freud began writing about it does not make the detour any less instructive.

The first psychoanalytic interpretation of a patient's suffering of which we have documented knowledge was made in Vienna in March 1881. It was Freud's medical colleague and early collaborator on hysteria, Josef Breuer, who was to treat the patient 'Anna O.' For two weeks, Anna O. had been completely dumb, unable to say a word. Breuer told her how he interpreted this: that he assumed that in some way or other she had been offended and had decided to herself not to talk about it. Breuer noted: 'When I guessed this and encouraged her to talk about it, the inhibition that had also made all other types of utterance impossible for her disappeared.'[4] What Breuer 'guessed' was that in order to maintain dumbness about one thing, the offence, Anna O. had decided, *subconsciously*, to become dumb about everything else as well, and so generalized her voluntary silence about something (the offence) into a universal, subconsciously desired silence.

Breuer's insight is just as simple as it is revolutionary: silence that is desired about one intention can lead to silence that is also desired about another, without the person being conscious of the fact. Breuer's insight leads directly to what psychoanalytic interpretations have as their special characteristic, what they are about: they are interpretations of intentions of which the subject of the interpretation (the patient) is unaware. Freud seizes on Breuer's insight, developing it into a theory about subconscious mental processes. The special thing about the interpretation that Breuer provided of Anna O. is that it does not base itself on an utterance at all. On the contrary, it is based on a non-act, a non-speaking, in a person who normally had a very great deal to say. But for the observant onlooker Anna's silence was paradoxically enough an equivalent of speech. Silence is eloquent, conspicuous; it is a symptom, it refers back to something, in other words it has a meaning. But what? The answer psychoanalysis suggests brings us one step closer to understanding the strange nature of psychic pain. Let us see what, broadly speaking, this answer is.

If the traditional story is true, it was the well-known French doctor J. M. Charcot who first inspired Freud to suspect that hysterical symptoms have a meaning. That which can be observed, the physical movements that can be read from the outside – the contractions, paralysis, trance – represent something else other than themselves. *They are something physical that refers to something mental.* If we take the hysterical symptoms of a woman whose husband is impotent, the idea is that there is a link between enforced sexual abstinence and a mental experience. Medical science prior to Freud distinguished between symptoms and causes: symptoms are ascribed to causes, and a treatment is prescribed that is directed towards the causes and not the symptoms. The point is that the symptom can be visible and recognized medically as an 'indication', or it can be reported as a subjective event, but in both cases a medical interpretation will ascribe a cause to it that is of the same type as the causes of physical illness.

Freud's great leap forward, inspired by Charcot and Breuer, consists in his not abandoning the doctrine of causality (that symptoms can be traced back to causes) but enlarging it to include a new area: the symptom does not need to be explained by a physical process, as do a tumour or an inflammation. The cause of the suffering (pathology) in the patient can be an event. 'Trauma', the original meaning of which was solely physical, understood as an injury, can now be used as a term for a causal event, but as an event it is a historical explanation: the patient is ill because something happened in the past, and what happened had a mental – psychological and emotional – significance from the very outset. While Charcot had used 'trauma' when talking about a physical injury that had a mental effect, Breuer and Freud used the term about an event that does not need in any way to be physical, but that has resulted in repression. Freud calls a trauma 'an event of incompatibility' or an experience, an idea or an emotion that has roused such a strong feeling of discomfort that the subject had decided to forget it. We are dealing here with impressions from the outside world that are so strong that they overwhelm and put out of action the ordinary defence and protection mechanisms of the self, as Freud formulates it in *Beyond the Pleasure Principle*.[5] A traumatic experience leaves behind a need on the part of the self to make an effort to refind its bearings, to be healed after the upheaval. According to Freud, this is a mental process that feeds on symbolic material, i.e. on the creation and integration of *meaning*.

What Freud makes us realize is that mental sufferings are caused by events that have made a strong (epoch-making) influence on the person. As far as the suffering (pathology) is concerned, however, it is not a question of the event as such but of the impression that arises in the patient's psyche. And such impressions do not need a physically and indubitably 'happened' event in order to be aroused, although it should at once be said that this is a controversial issue in psychoanalytic therapy, made topical by cases in recent years of individuals who claim to have been sexually abused (who indicate experiencing themselves as such, with accompanying symptoms in the form of emotional afflictions), but where there is considerable doubt as to whether actual or imaginary events underlie such claims. Mental sufferings –

and subsequent sufferings – can have a causal justification that, as far as other people can judge, is completely *without* correlating physical events (in the form of actual acts that are ascertainable facts in time and space, external and generally visible). Freud first assumed that patients had been exposed to real sexual assaults, that they 'were right' when they reported these as actual events. He later revised this theory (something he has been much criticized for), saying that the patients' accounts did not have physical correlatives in the form of actual events but only dealt with fantasy about events that were either strongly desired or strongly undesired. The important thing is that the fantasy – the mental content – in itself is causally sufficient to bring about, for example, a neurosis, i.e. a manifest mental affliction. It is this purely physical causality, its inner logic, that is the foremost discovery and theme of psychoanalysis in both a theoretical and therapeutic respect.

The causal connection we are dealing with exists between a past conflict situation – that which initially created the trauma – and the compulsively repeated reactions under which the person now suffers: the symptoms (in Anna O.'s case, the inhibition against talking freely that led to her not talking at all). The crucial idea, therapeutically speaking, is that when the source of the suffering is explained and understood, the actual fact that the individual gains insight into it – into what is creating the pressure that the symptoms are strategies for holding in check – contributes to the suffering being overcome. In other words, it loses its causal-determining power over the person's behaviour, e.g. in the form of compulsive thoughts and compulsive acts, often just as incomprehensible to the individual himself as to others, but that he, because of a violent inner pressure, feels 'compelled' to carry out, to repeat time after time.

It must of course be said that medical science, ever since the days of its pioneer Hippocrates, has been well aware that human nature is not restricted to what can be observed by examining the body. Every individual is the bearer of a history, *his own* history, and this history must always be taken into account when the individual's actual situation is to be understood, with the sufferings it may contain. An individual's earlier experiences are of invaluable importance for getting 'behind' the present sufferings and afflictions. What we are dealing with here is not what happened in a purely physical sense, that which is factual and can be confirmed and attested by everybody. No, it is what particular events have come to *mean* for the individual, what meaning the events have assumed and continue to exercize, maybe subconsciously rather than consciously. It is this highly subjective dimension of human exposure to pain that Freud points to via his original understanding of mental causality, i.e. that a person experiences something at the event level, is exposed to something that creates an inner impression, that latches onto the subconscious in a way that generates symptoms, that creates sufferings that are visible at the physical level, but whose triggering cause is mental.

Do not let me make this more cryptic than it is. Even though many of the assumptions and ideas of psychoanalysis are now considered speculative and unscientific, a great many of Freud's insights have become part of everyday language and the common understanding of our age. How then is it that Freud can help use to see what characterizes psychic pain as opposed to physical pain?

Man's reality is more than – does not coincide with – physical reality, that which the natural sciences study via observations and measurements. Man's primary reality is a mental reality. Only that which is mentally real for an individual is actually real. What, then, is this mental aspect?

As humans, we have no other conception of the world than that which is constantly transmitted by our memories, conscious and unconscious, about everything we have experienced during our entire lives. What plays a role – the decisive role – is not the objective or physical characteristics of what has happened, that has the nature of events and actions, but how the person experiences it, what meaning it assumes for him or her. 'Something' can only assume meaning for 'someone' because this 'someone', the human individual, is a mental being as well as a physical one. By 'mental' (= with a mind) I am referring to such things as 'experiencing things', 'gained experience', 'thoughts', 'feelings' and, above all, 'a person': all the former must be able to be connected to the latter, who is *the person* who has *them* (the experiences, thoughts, etc.). The primary characteristics of persons do not belong to the objects that exist in time and space outside persons.

The best example of what this implies is perhaps death. Persons are living physical beings that exist in time and space just like all other such beings. But we are – as far as can be ascertained – the only such beings that live conscious of the fact that our life will one day come to an end, that we shall die. Death – my certainty that *I* shall die, as the philosopher Heidegger emphasized – is a highly significant *mental reality* in my life long before it becomes a physical reality, something that actually happens to me. As a mental reality, death is a reality in my life that stands on its own two feet, separated from the nature of death as a physical event. Death means something particular for me *now*, even though its existence is in the form of not-being rather than being, of an experienced *not yet*. As persons we are beings that recall a past, not *the* past as such, or as something general, but *my* past, understood as the significance and meaning which that in the past, with which I exist in a (conscious and unconscious) experiential relationship, has acquired for me, and precisely for me as opposed to all other people, who may have 'taken part in' many of the same situations and events. Likewise, every one of us projects a future – not any future but *my* future, formed as ideas about it, hope for it, fear of it, plans for it, all of which, influenced by what my past has done to me, has predisposed me to – whether I will enter it with peace of mind or unease, erect or discouraged, hoping for the best or fearing the worst, made wise by good fortune or wise by adversity. The important here is that everything that has the nature of an event in a person's life is internalized by the person. Instead of things just 'happening' – happening in the world or happening to us – everything that has happened, is happening and may happen are taken inside us, populating our subjective world, equipping it with its 'mineness'. To be incorporated into this inner, subjective world means having the nature of what I call mental reality.

The concept of mental reality has aptly been summed up by Chateaubriand: 'Everyone bears within a world that consists of everything he or she has experienced and loved' – and hated or feared, I would add. The point is that we live at one and the same time in an outer and inner world; the *relation* between them is what is crucial: a relationship that in one person can be characterized by interactive flow and suppleness, in another by separation and rigidity. This notion of two worlds is not restricted to a psychoanalytical perspective; in fact it is a core element in all contemporary variations of object relations theory and theories of attachment. Each and every one of us, then, houses an inner world of thoughts, emotions and experiences: a world that consitutes my mental reality, and that brings together all fixing of meaning and significance. *Maturity* is characterized by a person's recognition of being dependent on good (real, outer) objects (i.e. persons, but also symbolic-cultural artefacts) that lend themselves to being introjected into the individual's inner world, thereby forming an invaluable source of positive meaning and self-awareness, while the temptation to assume control over such good inner objects is resisted. What does that mean? Why? Because – and this is a crucial insight, powerfully formulated by Melanie Klein and Donald Meltzer in particular – if we strive to take possession of our good inner objects, to have them at our disposal, their goodness, beauty and richness will be ruined. Only if these good inner objects are granted free passage, based on the conviction that they will not desert us, will they grant us their solicitude, their love, and thereby provide vital nourishment for our creativity, zest for life and working capacity.[6] In short, we are dependent on forces outside ourself that we cannot control; we remain vulnerable to the most important sources of experiencing that life is meaningful and that we are valuable. *Gratitude* is the attitude that corresponds to this realization.

An example of what I mean by psychic pain is mourning. Mourning is a cognitive and (not least) emotional reaction to loss. Mourning can invade a person to such an extent that everything that happens is blacked out by grief. Mourning is the state that synthesizes the world and all it contains for the mourning person; mourning is the 'organizing principle' that determines the value and meaning of everything encountered, in all thoughts, all feelings, all experiences. Life is lived in the hands of the mourning brought by loss, by bereavement. When the psychic pain released by, for example, the death of a dear one does not pass after a certain period of grief, when the person instead links his energy and his emotions to the lost object (the loved one), Freud speaks of healthy mourning turning into melancholy, i.e. a state typified by the person constantly dwelling on the past and cultivating the loss, and so blocking the person's ability to reengage with the world and to love anew.[7]

No matter whether we are speaking of sorrow or melancholy, it may sound as if these are states that control the person, rather than the reverse. Is that possible? Or is it really that sorrow only *apparently* controls the person? Does not sorrow only have the power it appears to have over the person on the condition that the person chooses to give sorrow such power?

Jean-Paul Sartre is famous, and notorious, for answering yes all the way. Sartre describes a time when he is sitting alone in a room, feeling sad. There is a knock at the door. I then, says Sartre, make 'an agreement with my sadness to leave it aside for a while and come back to it later', i.e. after the people visiting me have left. Since, according to Sartre, we 'don', put on, the emotion, we can also 'lay it aside' and resume it when the situation suits us better. For Sartre, this example shows how 'consciousness affects itself with sadness as a magical move against a situation that has become too troublesome'. As with other emotions, 'being sad means first making oneself sad'; sadness itself is a kind of behaviour that I choose.[8] Sartre presupposes a distinction between person and emotion, a distance that in every situation allows – or requires – the person to face his own emotion as a kind of object. So Sartre believes that I show, call back and modulate the emotion as something that is at my free disposal, that is in my sovereign power in the sense of being formable and determinable by me.

My disagreement with Sartre's view of emotions is important for understanding what I mean by psychic reality. When we examine what distinguishes physical pain from psychic pain, we must have a clear idea of what it is that has the nature of physical reality for us as persons. We have seen that physical reality arises and is maintained because of an effort on the part of the human subject: it is a question of how I as a person, with a highly individual life-history and with all the events and acts that are part of it, continuously *give meaning* to everything that has happened, is happening and may be going to happen. I am, then, an active interpreter of everything around me, everything that is part of my world, everything that is within my horizon; the mere fact that I interpret something to mean and signify something means that it assumes the nature of a mental reality for me. As a human, I am a being that is dependent on meaning. I am just

[margin annotation: We determine our own emotions and when we feel them]

42

as dependent on meaning in order to live as I am on food. I am hooked on symbolic nourishment. As far as we know, man is the only species that can become ill because of a loss of meaning, of not finding meaning or of only experiencing (interpreting) a meaning for that which occurs that is negative, that creates fear and, in the worst instance, destroys the zest for life. Without meaning I cannot live but not any old meaning will do. My existence depends on the meaning I manage to see *in* that which happens, that I come into contact with and am affected by. When I no longer have any clear idea of what means something and what something means, my very existence is threatened. I am of course in this world in the physical sense but in the psychic sense I am ailing and my physical survival depends on my psychic survival, which in turn depends on the access to meaning.

We are now ready to make the following assertion: psychic pain can be just as fatal as physical pain. Additionally, what causes psychic pain, what determines its seriousness, is far more complex and involves the individual's personality and life-history to a far greater extent than is the case with physical pain. As humans we are beings exposed to pain, although the exposure is of a very different kind when we are afflicted by psychic pain as opposed to physical pain.

Let me now provide a more detailed account of Sartre's position, with a subsequent critique, in order to clarify where that leads us.

FOUR

A Critique of Sartre's Existentialist View

Sartre is a so-called existentialist philosopher, one who I claim is in tune with the spirit of the present age. I am thinking in particular of Sartre's striking individualism, his emphasis of the fact that being a human being involves making choices, and that all of us make our choices in what is both total freedom and total aloneness: I and I alone am totally responsible for everything I do, and my freedom to choose cannot be de-chosen, rather, I am eternally sentenced to carry the responsibility that freedom involves, no matter how little that may appeal to me. In philosophical terms Sartre is a *voluntarist* because he places such emphasis on the freedom of the will in all our doings, the unique power of the will to determine meaning and significance for us.

Sartre's relevance for our theme consists in his assertion that my psychic reality is my own work and therefore completely my own responsibility. But have I not advanced precisely the same view above?

In fact my view differs from that of Sartre, and now we must look more closely at the resulting consequences in order to understand what psychic pain is.

For Sartre, feelings – like moods and mental states – are something chosen and willed by the individual. When, for example, some people claim that they 'were overcome with fear', Sartre's comment is that such people are what he would call 'in bad faith'. By referring to fear 'overcoming' them, they are attempting to escape from full responsibility for the way in which they acted in that situation. It is a question of presenting oneself as passive vis-à-vis the feeling and the mental state that was dominant, so that the stronger the feeling and state are asserted to be, the more the person will be in their power, be surrendered to them. Sartre reacts against such a view for two reasons. He believes that it is directly erroneous as a description of what actually happens, and that the description constitutes a highly questionable strategy from a moral point of view.

The truth is, Sartre maintains, that it is we who *make* ourselves passive in regard to our feelings, and on that basis we then renounce our responsibility for them, because of the (unpleasant) fact that we are the source of them and that feelings express judgements (judgements of value, to be more precise) about something or someone in the world that means something to us, that is not indifferent to us. According to Sartre's theory of emotions, we are always at a certain cognitive and will-based distance from them.[9] In short, a particular feeling (shame) or state (fear) is something we as persons decide to have, in the sense of 'assume', 'put on', in a given situation. Sartre is particularly interested in the fact that we assume feelings in order to tackle situations that seem threatening or troublesome to us. Feelings represent a kind of 'magic' – we use them to trick the situation, to make it less shameful, so that we can escape from it without losing face. In everyday social interaction with other people this is a strategy that is made frequent use of, more automatically as time goes on, without any appreciable awareness of what is happening; it is a strategy which we discover we can use with great success when with other people and that we allow others to use with great – though perhaps slightly less – success with us.

As I see it, there is something right about Sartre's analysis, but there is also something wrong, something that has consequences for our attempt to arrive at the distinctive nature of psychic pain. Sartre's conception gives us a good grasp of what can be called the cognitive dimension of feelings, i.e. that a particular feeling – shame, for example – is *about* something and in terms of judgement and value *has an opinion* about its object, since what the feeling refers to appears to be *meaningful*, in a positive or negative sense, to the subject. Sartre is good at depicting how the meaning and significance of a feeling are not to be considered neutral data in an objective world but instead are a dimension of the feeling (as with every experience) that is constituted by the subject, i.e. created and maintained by the subject as an intentional being, a being that actively has thoughts, feelings and a will-based initiative regarding everything encountered in its world.

But this does not catch all the dimensions of a feeling. For the strange thing about feelings, unlike thoughts and judgements and other characteristics of our cognitive abilities, is that they contain an *affective* dimension: the dimension of our being affected by them. And here I am not referring to affectedness in Sartre's one-sided sense of self-affectedness: that which a subject does to itself, including its own inner states, that which together populate and constitute his or her psychic reality. Via the affective dimension of the feeling I am rather in contact with a quality of *being* moved, shaken, hit, touched, as opposed to moving, shaking, hitting, touching (i.e. Sartre's position). In the feeling of shame and the state of fear I am precisely *in* the feeling and *in* the state, not facing it, as I face various objects in the world, in a relationship of externality to them, with the accompanying cleft between me on the one hand and the objects outside me on the other. Unlike that, I as a feeling, affected person am in an internal relationship with what the feeling or state is all about, with what it does to me, and with the whole particular world as presently disclosed to me by virtue of this feeling. As someone placed in shame or in fear I now *am* this shame and this fear, rather than someone who *has* them. The feeling defines me here and now, it marks the standing point from which I here and now sense and interpret everything in the world, everything that this special standing point in the world allows me to discover in it, given the horizon that comes with the point of world access and that bears its mark.

Sartre is without a doubt correct in saying that a feeling is always an interpretation, that we never feel anything particular in a cognitive vacuum (in terms of interpretation and evaluation). By placing all emphasis on the subject's interpretative contribution and responsibility for this, however, Sartre avoids answering the fundamental question as to what a feeling is, as distinguished from a thought or an act of cognition.

To use Sartre's example as an illustration: Sartre is right in saying that I *can* (try to) lay aside a particular feeling – the present feeling of sadness, for example, that I am so influenced by when sitting in the room as someone knocks at the door. But to point out that we can *behave* towards our sadness in this way is not the same as saying anything apposite about what the feeling – sadness – is. Sartre's many examples, despite being so vital and recognizable, only say something about how a person chooses to behave towards a particular feeling in a particular situation. The examples say nothing about the basic issue, i.e. what a feeling is. In other words, Sartre succeeds in saying something about the person who has the feelings, about the person's way of acting *towards* the feeling. But nothing has been said or shown about the feeling as such. It simply *is* there, like a fact in the world Sartre depicts (locates) the person as an observer of, and therefore always at a certain distance from. This means that Sartre loses sight of how the feeling arises. He loses what we could call the crude and the gut *firstness* of the feeling, the feeling such as I *am it* – am it as an affect, unlike some possible object for my thoughts and my will, with regards to what I, given the nature of the situation, can want to 'do' with it, e.g. suppress it or

47

inflate it. The feeling – seen in terms of affect as opposed to thought and evaluation – as I am in it is to be seen as prior to, indeed a prerequisite for, the *split* between me and my feeling, which is what Sartre bases himself on from start to finish. Sartre, we could say, begins the analysis of the feeling too late. He does not grasp its original affective dimension, as there is nothing that separates between me and my feeling. We are (in) the feeling before we observe it, objectify it; we *sense* the feeling (blushing, sweating) before we describe it, and before we eventually consciously go in for *doing* something particular with it. This entire cognitive dimension and its distinct work comes afterwards. When we are really seized by something, this means that we are moved, not that we move.

Admittedly, we must 'let' this object – this person, this situation – mean something to us; otherwise the being seized by it would not happen. This brings us to the absolutely crucial *ontological* point, that we have not chosen to be beings existing – living our lives – in such a way that we allow things to mean something for us, have meaning for us. That objects – events and acts, persons and situations – 'out there' mean something in an affective-moving sense is one aspect of our existence over which we do not exert choice. In the emotive response's *how* – that I feel so and not otherwise – my individuality towards the outside world and towards myself is foreshadowed, as Sartre rightly maintains, though at the cost of making this feature the most fundamental one. I answer for the response I display (jealousy, envy, shame) being *my* response, I vouch for it, it reflects me, says something about who I am, what is important for me, what is at stake for me in the particular situation. But – contra Sartre – the sensitivity, the affective susceptibility, that I am moved by how others are moved in a situation (via my capacity for empathy), is something about me that I *am*, not something I have chosen. Nor have I, as a human subject, decided all the modes of expression and manifestations of this sensitivity as they vary from one situation to the other (blushing as a bodily expression of my shame, sweating as an expression of my nervousness). Just as fully, I recognize these affective expressions as unmistakably *mine*.

And let me hasten to add: If I do *not* recognize myself, the distinctly personal, in my displayed repertoire of feelings, this is to be considered a sign of something being badly wrong with my self-relationship. In cases of fundamental non-recognition this is a symptom of psychopathology, of mental illness. From a clinical and therapeutic perspective, a far advanced ability, or even urge, or experience of coercion to lay aside an actual feeling (it could be shame, but also something positively charged, such as joy or pride) in order to take it up again later is not an innocent theoretical point about what it means to feel something (as Sartre believes). If anything, a person's urge to go in and out of his own emotional state, according to whatever for some reason or other (unconscious as well as conscious) is judged to be 'suitable' in the situation, can be a warning sign that the person is living out his feelings in an unauthentic way, more as an observer of them than one who completely *is* them. The more pronounced and persistent such a split between the person and the emotions is, the stronger the need for an explanation as to why things have become as they have in this person's life.

FIVE

Pain as a Phenomenon

I have discussed Sartre in order to make some progress towards gaining a good understanding of psychic pain. However, the question of what a feeling is, which we have dwelt on in Sartre's company, is not the question of what psychic pain is. What is the connection between them?

To begin with a simple answer: psychic pain is a feeling. Or put more generally: when I sense pain, I sense it as a feeling and when the pain is great, or its intensity violent and/or long-lasting, I experience pain as a state. That is the connection, at a basic level, between pain and feeling. Because there exists such an intimate connection between them, the points from the critical discussion of Sartre's theory about emotions can help us take the next step. If it is so (and who would protest?) that the way pain expresses itself is as a feeling, so that to be exposed to pain is the same as *being able to feel pain*, what difference does it make if the pain is physical or psychic?

Much would seem to indicate that the division between physical and psychic pain does more damage than good for an understanding of what pain is, although the division is so ingrained that I have not been able to avoid making use of it. The axe-blow to the leg is beyond a doubt an example of inflicted physical pain, as we have seen earlier. But, as we also saw, how I interpret this situation plays an important role in my experiencing of this (physical) pain; I give it a meaning in my situation, I fear that it will stop me carrying out certain plans I had made, I experience that the injury bothers me and that it ruins my good mood. It would be possible to go on giving examples like this of my leg injury, despite the fact that seen from the outside, considered in isolation and from a medical point of view it is 'only' a matter of – fully curable – physical pain, *it pains me* in ways that break with and go far beyond its purely physical nature. As a definitively entered constituent of my mental reality even the simplest physical injury (or somatic affliction) is an event in my life that always has more dimensions than the physical. In other words, even the simplest physical injury has a *meaning* for the person injured. And the question of what the meaning more precisely consists of obliges us to shift focus from the physically describable (and medically manipulatable and curable) side of the injury to the role the injury plays as a mental reality in the injured person.

When I claim that the way in which we 'have' pain as human beings is via *feeling* pain, via the full sensing of it, that means that the feeling of pain cannot be separated from the conscious understanding (cognition) of pain. The principal characteristic of pain is precisely the feeling of something causing pain.

Let us make use of the insights we arrived at in the discussion of Sartre. He claims that as human subjects we always choose the quality of our experience, including the actual feeling we might have, and consequently we are free to de-choose it, to exchange it with a different feeling that will contain a different interpretation, a different strategy for mastering the situation. Against this, I assert that pain is particularly suitable for demonstrating that there are feelings and states that we are obliged to live with and that we therefore are not in a position to go in and out of at will. In a fundamental sense, the feeling of pain is not a product of thought. The feeling of pain has an autonomy, an independence and sovereignty vis-à-vis the person who senses it. If we ignore situations where persons more or less intentionally inflict pain on themselves, and that form the exception (I shall address phenomena of that type in a later chapter), we have to say that the rule is that pain comes and goes independently of human thought and will. The reality of pain is the reality of the feeling of pain, its persistence, its entry into my life-world, its nature of being an uninvited guest, or should we rather say intruder, one that comes without my wanting it or having thought of it being thus, and that does not go away even though I might wish for it more than anything else. Pain possesses an utterly sovereign power, a sovereignty that marks the limit for my belief in my own power, my freedom and my determining right over everything in my life, over all its significance and meaning. Pain heaves the ego down from the pedestal.

Against this (call it 'phenomenological') background, we can see that physical and psychic pain can indeed be separated from each other purely analytically and as regards theoretical discussion. But it would be contrary to the experienced nature of pain – and it is pain as something experienced that interests us, for how else are we to approach it, to be able to say anything about it? – to hold onto a strict division between the psychic and the physical when examining the experience of pain, i.e. what it means to have pain. Common to all types of pain, no matter their actual causes (etiology), is that pain has to do with hurting, that *hurting* is what the feeling is quintessentially about. As we touched on in the discussion of Freud and psychoanalysis, bodily pains (symptoms of a somatic nature) can originate in mental or psychological (emotional) factors. Anna O. suffered (probably, if the story is true) from enforced sexual abstinence in relation to her husband. The mental and emotional meaning of living in this situation, i.e. in a situation of subjectively interpreted, felt and suffered dissatisfaction, dissatisfaction regarding something to which the person Anna O. attached great importance, leads to an affliction that has physical as well as psychological symptoms. The general point is that pain moves in both directions: psychic pain can be caused by bodily-physical factors, just as physical pain can be provoked by mental causes. Psychic pain can bring about as well as intensify physical pain, and vice versa.

This assertion entails a particular view of the body's role in relation to pain. Because I am my body, because my body is me, the pain in my leg as a result of the axe-blow is not a product of my thought, my interpretation or my will. Simply as hit by the blow and hence as addressed by the pain immediately and inadvertently accompanying the blow, I cannot *not* relate to it. In being hurt I am affected by and involved in something non-optional and non-voluntary. Just as little as my feeling has primarily been given me as an object among other objects in the world can I have such an objectifying distance from the painfulness which I sense is located in one of my limbs. In a full sensuous-experiential sense, I *am* where the pain comes from, its enforced here-and-now, its peculiar way of centering my world, even (sometimes, as we shall see below) shirking it; I am not outside this brought-about painfulness and at a distance from it. *I am the pain in my body because I am that body.* And I cannot otherwise have a world, be in the world, in the manner characteristic of humans.

The French philosopher Maurice Merleau-Ponty, upon whom I draw here, puts it like this: 'My body is not only an experience among many. It is the yardstick of everything, the reference point for all the world's dimensions.'[10] My body is not an object. While I am able to leave all objects in the world, in the sense that that I can influence and manipulate their presence and absence, my proximity to or distance from them, I cannot leave my body. It defines my being-in-the-world by determining and demarcating the standing point from which I at any time sense, think, feel and move around in the world. Where I am, my body is; where my body is, there am I.

That pain is corporeal does not say much. It only says something about its localization: that it is mine, that it has me as its residence. When experiencing physical pain, my awareness of the pain will vary, depending on the nature of the pain; pain can come and go, be transient or lasting, even chronic. Pain can grant me a break, allow me to fetch myself in again and regain some strength, or it can hold me in a grip of steel that never relaxes and is perhaps constantly being tightened. Generally speaking, pain is what makes the body a particularly important concern for the individual. The fact that the body, often quite suddenly and unprepared for by me, becomes a place for a concentration of pain, forces me to have a new relationship with my own body. Merleau-Ponty is one of those who has pointed out that it is because of pain (illness, injury, dysfunction) that I become aware of my body at all. Normally, especially as long as I am still young, I do not want to 'know about' my body. Obviously, I am keenly aware of it in certain situations and in connection with particular experiences – sexual ones are perhaps the best example – but as a rule I will not have my attention fixed *on* my body. If anything – in the spirit of Merleau-Ponty – I will in all my activities, actions, experiences and plans sense, feel, and act *with my body*, my body as the self-evident, unreflected and unnoticed centre in the sequence of everything I happen to do, experience, feel, want, etc. My body is not among the things or themes in the world I 'take in', focus my attention on. On the contrary, my body is the actual condition of possibility that I am located as I am in the world at all, am active, movable in this way, that I can focus my attention and energy on anything at all of what exists outside me (outside my body).

This is what is so dramatically changed, even turned upside-down, from the moment the body becomes a centre for pain. *Pain steals the focus.* Pain commands my total attention, it drains me of energy, it demands everything of me, finally more than I am able to give – it wears me out. Pain is voracious: it wants to consume me, have all of me, not share my consciousness, my thoughts, feelings and will with any-one or anything else. Pain is intensely jealous: it eliminates all rivals of my attention and energies as soon as they emerge, so that finally all that is left is pain, as the all-consuming and all-penetrating centre of my life. I am pain, the pain is me, there is nothing else, nothing outside. Admittedly, I can attempt to use cunning, to protest. I can attempt to take a mental time-out from it, to rest from it so as to make it leave me in peace. But where pain is intense enough, pervasive and long-lasting enough, the thought of – as well as other people's well-meant advice to try – 'thinking of something else' is nothing more than an ineffectual gesture that does no good at all, being thoroughly impotent. Pain catches up with me, reminds me where I belong and have to stay put: at home, at home with my body, *in* my body, *as* my body. Absence of distance – or better: distancelessness – is what physical pain at its most intense is all about, ineluctably at that; it is how such pain works, as it were. When experiencing severe pain my entire life-world, my horizon, is narrowed down; my perception of time and space, my relations with other people as well as with myself are dramatically changed. The final point is reached when existence is reduced to the body. That which was pos-sible as something self-evident and calling only for a minimum of effort becomes impossible. The eminent and apparently limitless, unforced and unhindered openness to the world of the senses, the openness to everything it might contain, is replaced by a solid closure. The outward-looking nature of the senses, their levity and mobility, their non-stop curiosity towards everything and everyone, not least what-ever might seem to be new and unfamiliar, worth pausing and looking at, everything that enables, maintains and inten-sifies our actual contact with the world, our engrossment in it, withers away. Like muscles that atrophy when not used, our hearing will decline and our gaze become limited. Nursing scientist Per Nortvedt, speaking of patients with severe pain, puts the characteristic alteration of their world-experience like this: 'The room I am placed in is emptied of content, it becomes cramped, impossible to gain an overview of, not because of some objective features of the room, physically speaking, but because one does not have the strength to look at what is there. One sees and yet does not see, because one does not have the strength to see.'[11]

Painfulness thus creates a distance from everything except the pain itself. Pain is like a magnet that attracts all attention, all energy, towards itself. At the same time as all attempts at openness towards the world outside are killed at the moment of birth, are strangled by pain's never-resting presence, pain does not allow itself to be shut out. Pain becomes a tyrant, an all-organizing centre in the person's consciousness, sensuality and physicality, something that mercilessly dictates all significance, all meaning. The life-world of the person shrinks to this single hub; one is powerless and surrenders totally to the omnipotence of pain. If pain becomes completely autonomous, the person in its power becomes completely heteronomous, under alien control. And here, in keeping with what existentialist philosophers like Martin Heidegger help us to appreciate, loss of (outside) world means loss of self; the former assumes the form of the latter, the two becoming experientially indistinguishable. For even if the pain is unmistakably *mine*, no one else's, it forces me to abandon myself, my determining of what I will do and what has meaning to me. I experience it as if something alien and deeply hostile has taken up residence in me. I am consumed from the inside; the outer limits of my body to the world no longer help me to keep out what is threatening and unpleasant. No, the opposite applies: the limits of my body as a marker of my separateness from everything else and everybody else in the world makes any retreat from that which hurts in the world possible for me, since my body is now the vessel that keeps the pain inside, that ensures that it becomes lasting in me, as that which defines my entire existence. In philosophical terms this means that the pain by means of its body-located reality transforms my whole being into *immanence*, since every attempt to go beyond (transcend) it becomes impossible.

The phenomenological perspective I have adopted, following Merleau-Ponty, is well suited to explain how pain, if it is particularly intense and long-lasting, transforms my sense of myself as a body, as existing in the world as a corporeal being. The more unbearable my bodily pains are, the more fundamentally my entire existence is reduced to the physical. But what about pains that do not have so strong a localization in the physical?

We have touched on the form of causality that deals with how something purely physical can cause – be sufficient cause of – something physical, in the form of somatic-corporeal suffering. That a physical change (dysfunction, inhibition, injury) can be effected by something non-physical, that something somatic can be effected by something non-somatic, something corporeal by something non-corporeal, is an insight that goes right back to Hippocrates, the father of medicine, but of which Sigmund Freud in particular has influenced our modern understanding. The question we need to examine, however, is whether we can talk about a purely mental causality as far as pain is concerned, in such a way that a cause of a mental nature can bring about a purely mental effect, in the form of psychic pain.

SIX

Anxiety and Depression

Anxiety and depression are two especially salient instances of psychic pain. Let us explore what is distinctive about them.

While fear is a feeling with a particular object in the world, where the person experiencing fear has a clear idea of what he fears (the object of fear), anxiety is different. To have anxiety – or, more precisely, to be *in* anxiety – is to find oneself in a state where the cause is unknown to the person experiencing it. While fear is in principle easy to tackle because of the possibility of removing or in some other way taking action against its object, with anxiety no such easy options or exits are available. Many philosophers within what is loosely labelled existentialist thought, including Kierkegaard, Heidegger and Sartre, have devoted much attention to the experience of anxiety (*Angst*). The assertion is that anxiety has a potential to rouse the individual to a new, deeper insight into his own life: to realize that this is *my* life, these are *my* possibilities, and it is *my* responsibility to assume these possibilities and make the best of them, and to answer for the choices I make as those that reflect what sort of a person I wish to be. Anxiety is the royal road to a privileged recognition of the fact that I am obliged to adopt an attitude to universal and general characteristics of each human being's existence in the world in *my* way. As Heidegger says, anxiety can rouse me to a recognition of the fact that it is not first and foremost a question of *one* being mortal but that *I* shall die. Anxiety individualizes what otherwise is held at arm's length by being viewed as universally human, by being generalized and thus having its sting removed, its nature of a challenge to *me* personally, for example, the marking by mortality of an absolute limit for all *my* projects. As humans, all of us are mortal. But only I can live – interpret, tackle, count on – *my* mortality: no one else can do it for me, no more than I can step in for other people.

It is in the spirit of existentialism to ascribe to anxiety what I here will call a characteristic pathos of genuineness. Sartre and Heidegger talk about authenticity (*Eigentlichkeit*). Anxiety brings me back home to myself. It forces me to be confronted with myself, with the normally so obscured, overlooked and repressed fact that the only instance for ascribing meaning and significance – of everything that constitutes mental reality – in my life is myself. Thus anxiety and the experience it provides is in stark contrast with my everyday existence. This is dominated by a mentality that tells me that significance and meaning are something that is *received*, something I regularly meet up with and that falls into my lap when encountering objects in the world and by virtue of all my experiences. I think about things in the way that *one* (*das Man*) thinks about them; I experience as good what *one* experiences as good; I fear what *one* fears (alluding here to Heidegger's famous analysis in *Being and Time* of everyday-ness and the conformity it supposedly entails) – and I do so in the same fashion and for the same reasons as everyone else does; for that is what I assume they do, just as others assume that I experience the same in the same way as they do.[12] In short, everything that has to do with meaning and significance is received passively by me on my journey through life, in all I meet up with and am exposed to.

It must be said that not much effort is required to spot weaknesses in this conception of the origin of meaning. However, the point is not to present it as a robust philosophical position. It is rather to see how and why anxiety – anxiety more than anything else – can give rise to the outlined *one*-fixated mentality being broken and subsequently rejected.

What happens in anxiety? Anxiety typically comes abruptly, completely without warning. The culturally favoured metaphors are those of being ambushed by a violent and unexpected force, nay, enemy: anxiety conquers me, tears me to shreds. It can wear me out, drain my energy. It can be experienced as a battle, where anxiety is my enemy, the stranger in my midst who knocks me down, who springs up without my being able to prevent or control it. I can try taking up the battle, mobilizing my energy to outwit the anxiety, conquering it, neutralizing it. I can try avoiding the paths where it lies in wait, playing 'safe', avoiding provocations.

But a life spent pussyfooting around, where all my doings are low key so as not to awaken and get embroiled in anxiety, is just as much a life in anxiety's power. When anxiety has first announced its arrival, it is as if I do not have a chance of warding off its attack. It is in command. Gradually, I can best describe my situation as completely characterized by *a fear of anxiety*, of its presence and the suffering this presence inflicts on me. Anxiety is thus the perhaps most unadulterated version of psychic pain. When all of me is 'just anxiety', when anxiety is all I am, when everything that exists exists within anxiety and is contaminated by it, when nothing outside it is sensed and has meaning, then anxiety has become one with my psyche. Having merged with me and all I sense, feel and can think of, being one with me and all that I experience, anxiety is no longer separable from my bodily being either. Anxiety paralyses my corporeal-sensual openness towards the world. It hampers my movements, and it may force me to make certain movements – in the form of rituals, often taking on a most exhausting because compulsory nature – that I feel dictated to do, and precisely in the detailed and rigid manner required by it, at that, no deviations, no small freedoms allowed me. The movements and acts I carry out compulsively grant me the prospect of a certain quietude, a time-out in the maelstrom of anxiety. While the break is only temporary, obeying the dictates of anxiety and scrupulously doing as it dictates does not give me any victory over it, does not liberate me from it, but merely serves to consolidate its almost total power over me.

What we are seeing here is that anxiety does to me what we earlier saw that painfulness can do. Even though anxiety can be cultivated in its purely mental aspects, and even though the painfulness we discussed earlier can have a purely physical injury as its triggering cause, this contrast between a mental and physical origin is of virtually no importance with a view to how the pain behaves. The phenomenological and experientially oriented analysis yields almost identical results in both cases.

In the significance existentialist philosophy grants to anxiety there lies, however, a message of a positive nature. How is that possible? Has what we have said about the nature of anxiety not been exclusively negative?

When anxiety is portrayed as a royal road to a novel and deeper recognition of a person's responsibility for his own life and own choices and possibilities, we are dealing with a potential in the experiencing of anxiety that can seem to be positive. Anxiety is understood something that more than anything else *rouses* the individual to take responsibility for and in his own life. This is particularly the case in Heidegger, since he links anxiety to 'the call of conscience', a call that contains an exhortation to stop living in the power of non-self-sameness, typified in terms of thoughts and acts by what *one* does and regards as being important and right, in conformity with what is established, practised and executed without reflection. Anxiety forces me to have it out with such 'other-orientation', to use the concept of the sociologist David Riesman.[13] Anxiety throws me into my own arms, throws me back with great violence from the concerns of others, from everything outside me and the 'inherent' significance and meaning I have more or less passively received and adopted. Anxiety creates an opening, in the final instance an abyss, between me and everyone else, between me and the world in which others exist, see the significance of and find meaning in. For the fact is that I do not do so – not any more, not after anxiety has entered the scene. Now there are two lives, that prior to anxiety and that since. I have lost the connection between them. I am fumbling for the way back, but have to acknowledge that nothing can be as it was before.

Out of the existential distress into which anxiety casts me unawares hope arises – a possibility for change. Anxiety has such a potential because it takes the form of *experience*. Experience (*Erfahrung*) is something else than 'an' experience (*Erlebnis*). Anxiety is the reference point of existence – anxiety is human discomfort and alienation in this world *par excellence*. Anxiety is this *void*, that which I am simply in but cannot point to, cannot objectify, make into something outside me and that I thereby can distance myself from and control. I can no more distance myself from the body than I can distance myself from anxiety. Both define and determine the possibilities and limits of my existence, what I am and what I can do. Once anxiety lodges itself in the body – which is what it does, for it does not let anything that is me go free – the body is permeated by anxiety. What then?

We have hitherto depicted the way into anxiety, but not said a word about the way out. To do that, we must examine more closely the assertion that anxiety is experience. What is experience? Experience in the German-inspired (as it were) sense intended here, is a tremor, a shock. I am struck by what is happening to me; it changes my view of the world. Experience takes me out of the familiar, smooth flow of existence. Experience introduces a break, a radical discontinuity, into my life, causes an upheaval. What was formerly familiar to me is no longer so, or no longer means anything to me. But experience does not only represent such negativity, such a stimulus of a break and of something new. It also contains elements of what is necessary for me to establish new meaning, find a new foothold. So experience opens me up towards the world, it enables, indeed even promotes, *transcendence*, the going beyond the given, the usual and the familiar. Experience is subversive in challenging and not leaving unaltered what is (felt, thought, done, planned); it is revolutionary in paving the way for something completely novel and unknown, promising a new beginning: that my existence in the world start afresh.

Experience, then, can turn anxiety into something else than mere negativity, unadulterated painfulness. That is how Heidegger sees it.[14] By anxiety containing a call of conscience, it instils an experience that forces me to make a new departure. And by the nature of things, this departure is felt – experienced – as something unpleasant, unwanted – in short, as painful. As the ancient Greeks pointed out – and as Heidegger later reminded people – there is a strong affinity between pain and experience. Experience cannot be anything else than painful. Pain signals the sting of experience, the challenge it confronts me with: the challenge to scrutinize myself, to recognize and fully accept that no other instances than myself can establish *meaning for me* in this life, since there is no *meaning in itself*. To take the consequences of this new departure, this waking to assuming responsibility for ascribing meaning as well as all acts and choices I might make is something that creates anxiety. But – paradoxically enough – it is at the same time the task that anxiety – and in a privileged sense – prepares the ground for in me, that it sets me in motion towards being *able* to assume. In other words, anxiety has a dual function in this picture: on the one hand, it rouses the person to assume responsibility in the mentioned (strictly individual) sense; on the other hand, the discomfort regarding such a responsibility can intensify the anxiety. So anxiety is not simply something that paralyses; by containing a call to assume responsibility for my own life and all my choices, it also has a truly rousing and so constructive effect.

To what extent anxiety is rousing is very much open to discussion. For a start, both the person plagued by anxiety and the professionals who treat people with anxiety will more probably confirm its paralysing than its rousing effect. As far as the aspect of meaning is concerned, it is just as common to see anxiety as emptying things of the meaning they once had, as sabotaging the assignment of meaning rather than enabling it. I do not deny that this is so – nor does Heidegger. Indeed, we should acknowledge that anxiety contains more elements than those most striking from a clinical point of view – say, the psychiatrist's. From a philosophical perspective, there are without a doubt grounds for claiming that anxiety can be a benchmark in a person's life, that it can mark a great upheaval, make life go out of control and turn everything upside-down – and that precisely because of this negativity, this undermining of everything that was, it contains the germ of a new beginning. On the other hand, anxiety can extract so much energy from the person involved that there is none left to take up the gauntlet which, as Heidegger says, has been thrown down in the form of a 'call of conscience' – to give a realistic clinical corrective to Heidegger's analysis. The philosophical point that anxiety is a type of experience that contains such a – positive, innovative – potential, is valid, even though statistics might indicate that the paralysing effect is greater than the rousing effect. For many people, the confrontation with themselves, with their own wounds as well as with the most difficult sides of life that anxiety has brought about, may have produced greater self-insight and encouraged that a different future course be chosen. There are many ways out of the darkness of anxiety. But to find them and have enough strength to set out on them, a person needs allies – allies in both a physical and symbolic sense. For anxiety does not itself provide the resources required for leaving it behind. Anxiety may rouse one to heightened awareness of *the necessity* of wrestling with one's own life, abandoning conformist or rigid ways of feeling and thinking and helping a person to discard inauthentic goals and reject false values. But still it is only I who, when all is said and done, can save myself from anxiety. The fact that I *myself* have to find the way out of anxiety, pull myself up out of it by the hair, can of course intensify the anxiety. In such cases, anxiety – or rather the constant reference to anxiety as paralysing – functions as a kind of cushion, a 'reason' for my not getting any further. As is often pointed out, not least by person's talking from firsthand experience, anxiety is anxiety's worst enemy – the fear of its enduring embrace can contribute to its precisely tightening its paralysing grip.

There is, however, a more profound question that needs to be addressed. On several occasions I have observed that to be a human being means to ascribe meaning and significance to everything around us, and that each and every person has a responsibility to do this, and to vouch for the meaning – the interpretations, evaluations and priorities – that results. In short, meaning is actively created, not received; it is created from the subject outwards, not from the objects inwards; meaning has the nature of being something *for me*, not something *in itself*.

This way of seeing things – that of existentialist philosophy if you like – contains important insights; moreover, I believe it is strongly represented in the thinking of the present age. But it does not tell the *whole* story of humanity and pain. As will become clear later, the question of the nature of pain, its meaning and significance, is not *only* a subjective concern, something that is decided on by the individual subject. No, the question forces us in addition to dwell on the characteristics of the pain phenomenon as such, characteristics of the reality of pain that are as they are independently of the subject's abilities to decide things. Over and above looking more closely at the particular nature of the phenomenon (pain), the contribution of society – or in my terminology, culture – must be recognized as being highly important for how the individual interprets and tolerates pain in his own life and in that of other people.

Let me begin by correcting Sartre. We recall Sartre's assertion that I choose my own feeling. He claimed this on the basis of a theory about feelings that implies that we as persons are in a separate, outward and manipulative relation to our feelings. So it is up to each and every one of us to modulate – to give appearance, form and content to – the feeling we display in a given situation. Sadness, we recall, can be annulled; I can come back to it when my visitor has left and the situation once more makes sadness appropriate, i.e. when it does not involve a loss of face or in some other way make me feel embarrassed.

As we recall, I rejected these implications of Sartre's theory. A central argument was that we find ourselves in an internal and pre-reflective – as opposed to an external and manipulative – relation to the feeling we actually have. We have the feeling by being it, being fully and completely present in it, and thus stamped by it. I am not the one who forms the feeling; it is the feeling that – precisely here and now – forms me, gives a direction to my way of 'taking in' the world, of sensing it in a broad sense. Heidegger talks in this connection of *attunement* (*Befindlichkeit*), i.e. that a feeling places me in a particular mode in terms of mood, senses and interpretation, determining my receptiveness towards the world, what I notice and the way I do so. We could crudely say that while Sartre wants the feeling to be *in front of* me, for it to have the nature of an object and be capable of being manipulated in the way external objects can in principle, Heidegger shows that the feeling, with the specific mode of atmosphere it is part of, is *behind* me; I am not at a distance from it, but am controlled by it as something 'at the back', something I am one with, something that determines how I sense and see the world, but which I myself cannot see. It is a way of being in the world.

When we changed focus from feelings in general to the state of anxiety in particular, we saw, however, that Heidegger strongly emphasizes the role he believes *choice* plays. The positive, creative potential of anxiety understood as experience consists in the possibility of the person in anxiety being able to be roused to assume responsibility for his life, a responsibility for his or her actually being the one who – alone – constantly *chooses* what is to have meaning (be important or unimportant) and what meaning various events, phenomena and actions are to have. So we arrived at the conclusion that meaning is always *for me*.

What has happened? A certain shift has taken place. While Sartre claims that I choose the feeling as such, Heidegger rejects this (and rightly so), only to claim later on that in the particular feeling constituted by anxiety, *there* I do choose, there I show my true face – and precisely because my self-sameness and authenticity are at stake here (what I show myself capable of, or avoid, and thereby continue to live and life of non-self-sameness), anxiety acquires such an existential seriousness, such a pathos of genuineness, as I called it earlier. In short, the choice shifts from the feeling to anxiety, from having to apply to all feelings as such (Sartre) to applying to – be an enabled experience of – the distinct feeling of anxiety. Correctly understood (in Heidegger), I do not choose anxiety as such; instead, it could be said that I am *in anxiety*, or as 'an anxious person' am in a position to make my most crucial decisions, decisions that say something profound and genuine about who I am and seek to be. Anxiety is a springboard for existentialist choices, for my taking on *my* possibilities and thereby assuming responsibility for my life. That raises the question of whether this emphasis on choice, on the possibility of being able to choose, and choose freely, can be defended at a closer look. This is an important question for our theme, because it sheds light on pain: is pain something we can choose, insofar as pain (in one of its dimensions at any rate) is to be considered a feeling?

Without dwelling further on what the answer looks like for Sartre and Heidegger, my claim is that we are not free to choose the pain we feel, and thereby to de-choose it. We do not have the reality of pain, the difference between its presence and absence at our disposal. Nor is it up to me (and my capacities as an intentional subject, capable of thought, will and emotion) to determine the intensity of pain, if it is strong or weak, temporary or lasting, keen or just a dull ache.

SEVEN

The Unalterable Fundamental Conditions of Existence

But is this answer not inadmissibly general, bordering on the platitudinous? And who is likely to disagree? Is this not something everybody knows and can readily agree with? There is nothing wrong in claiming something that is generally accepted as being true. However, this general consideration is not the whole story as regards pain on the one hand and freedom of choice on the other.

Feelings in general and their affective aspect in particular reveal the ontological dimension of human existence, pointing to the *given* and the *unalterable*, i.e. the non-choosable, about certain fundamental conditions of existence. Feelings relate us to, bring us into contact with and to recognition of aspects of existence over which we have no control. According to my view, feelings are not only *about*, i.e. directed towards, something that shows the limits for our control and our freedom. Feelings as such, especially the most basic ones, also reveal something uncontrollable *in ourselves*, namely our existence as affectable and hence violable beings.

Dependence, vulnerability, mortality, the fragility of relations and existential loneliness: these are examples of the unalterable fundamental conditions of life. That we are thrown into a world with a dependence (on food, on the care of others, on meaningful experiences, etc.) we can never completely detach ourselves from, and with death as that which finally makes all our possibilities impossible (Heidegger), means that we live our lives in insurmountable vulnerability.

That we live our lives under the givenness of these fundamental conditions is a fact, one that applies to each and every
one of us. *How* we live – in the sense of relating to these fundamental conditions and their unalterable givenness – does,
on the other hand, vary from one person to the next. What
applies to all of us here is that we cannot live the fundamental conditions in a neutral way. The many answers to the
question of 'how' are so many ways – individually distinct
ways – in which we live the fundamental conditions. *The reality of the fundamental conditions is, then, general, whereas the
way in which we handle them is individual.*

To grasp where this leads us, consider anxiety. Anxiety reduces me to a zero point: a state where nothing any longer has
any meaning, where everything becomes flat, grey, indistinguishable. This particularly applies when anxiety is part of a
depression. When I have been reduced to such a zero point, such
a darkness, everything that has to do with the meaningful has
to be created anew. Within existentialism this is considered
a unique opportunity for me to generate all meaning out of
myself, to look straight in the eye the unpleasant and normally
repressed fact that it is not the world as such, or society, or the
others that continually create, maintain and communicate
meaning, but myself.

What is peculiar about the unalterable fundamental conditions
I introduced, however, is that they cannot be chosen. They mark
the limit of what I can determine shall or shall not be: the fundamental conditions are real, whether I wish it or not. They constitute a framework within which I have to live. According to
Heidegger, anxiety can rouse me to a recognition of my mortality,
as we have seen. I see that I have to adopt an attitude, in my freedom, in my individuality, to something that I have not brought
about myself and am unable to remove. Understood thus, it is
a question of freedom as insight into necessity: freedom as the
conscious assumption of responsibility for *how* I live – tackle –
the characteristics of my existence that cannot be chosen.

Sartre has a different view of this, which has consequences for the understanding of pain. In his major work *Being and Nothingness* Sartre uses the following example. I go for a walk in the mountains along with some friends. After walking for several hours we approach our first destination; there is only a long uphill slope left before we are at the top, which we can glimpse up there. Halfway up the last ascent I suddenly throw myself down on the path, fling away my rucksack and exclaim: 'I can't go any further, I can't take another step – we've got to stop here!' My fellow hikers are amazed and ask me why. I produce a long list of reasons why I cannot continue: how many hours we have been walking, how long it is since we have taken a rest and drunk any water, how steep the ascent is, how hot it is, how heavy my rucksack is. And so on and so forth. The others reply that they do not want to stop now, that they have walked just as far as I have, that they are carrying as much as I am, that they are just as thirsty. Why should *I* not be able to carry on? By means of this example, Sartre wishes to show what it means to be in 'bad faith'. When I offer this long list of objective facts – the length of the trip, the weight of the rucksack, the steepness of the ascent – as *reasons* why I absolutely 'have to' give up at this point, I am placing everything that explains and motivates my action in conditions outside myself, in circumstances. I present things as if the circumstances, or the sum of their effect on me, dictate my action. In short, I refuse to recognize that I have a choice, that the action I am taking reflects *me*, my free subjectivity, rather than being a kind of determined product of a series of objective and impersonal circumstances.

Sartre insists that my not being able to go any further is a totally free – a completely chosen – act on my part. All the reasons I advance can be considered equivocations: they betray my strategy to flee from the responsibility for the act, to deny my freedom as the principle that solely determines all my actions. For to act *is* to choose, and to choose *is* to be free – it is how freedom manifests itself in the world. It follows from Sartre's position that I as a subject, as consciousness, completely decide the meaning of pain – for example in a situation where I notice that I am tired. When I then say: 'I can't go on', what happens is that I *decide* that I can't go on. I choose myself as a person who in this situation cannot go on, while my fellow hikers on the other hand choose themselves as persons who can go on – we make opposite choices in the same situation.

Sartre's assertions regarding the example he provides are persuasive. Even so, I do not think he gives us a convincing analysis of the reality of pain in human existence. Why not? As we recall from Sartre's theory about feelings, he presupposes that we are always at a distance from our feelings. When I walk in the mountains and notice that I am becoming more and more exhausted, until I suddenly throw myself down and cannot take 'a single step further', Sartre assumes that I am at a distance from my state, in the form of my experienced fatigue, that my powers are exhausted, that my thirst is intolerable, as is the heat. His assertion is that *I* – nothing else, no one else – am the one who completely, from beginning to end, determine my weariness, i.e. my present state.

The question it is important to clarify is this: Do I decide *that* I am exhausted, or do I decide what *meaning* the fact I am tired out is to have – for example, in the form of my lying down and being unable to take a step further? The more radical point of view is, of course, the first one, namely the claim that I decide I am exhausted, or, to put it more generally, that I am totally free, and therefore totally responsible, for every state I might happen to find myself in and every feeling I might happen to have. The alternative, that I unfold my freedom and my responsibility with regard to the specific meaning of the state I am in, represents a far more moderate view.

My suggestion is that pain is particularly well suited for demonstrating that Sartre's position – interpreted in the first alternative – is untenable. And not simply that. It is also possible to challenge the moderate version of the position when we focus on pain. For pain is not just any state or feeling. As I have pointed out, pain is characterized by its lack of distance, by its directness: my pain fills me, marks me, with an immediacy and permeability that are in stark contrast to Sartre's analysis. Let us assume that Sartre admits this. Can he not just as well insist that I, the one who has the pain, decide its meaning – for how else is the meaning otherwise to be determined? In short, is Sartre's assertion not saved that I am the one who completely decides that my pain is *unbearable*, and thereby also decide – in the sense 'choose' – the consequences I allow this to have, e.g. that I do not take another step?

No, I do not believe that this – more moderate – assertion can be maintained on a closer look at what sort of phenomenon pain is for us humans. Pain does something to us, changes and transforms us, and the reality of this aspect of experiencing pain – that pain is an experience in the strict sense that strikes and shakes us and causes everything to be altered – is lost in Sartre's insistence on freedom and choice.

EIGHT

Transportation of Psychic Pain

My main idea is that *pain belongs to human life,* as opposed to Sartre's idea that the person – continuously and freely – gives (this or that) meaning to pain. Certain forms of pain – or more precisely, inflictions of pain – are of such a nature that pain destroys all meaning: everything that had been established as meaningful, as secure, from earlier on, as well as every prospect of finding new meaning in the future, *after* what has now happened. It can be felt as a threat to all meaning in one's existence that one is suddenly struck down by a serious illness or accident, or that those close to one are. An even harder assault on meaning in life, security in the world and trust in it takes place when a person is exposed to outrages from others without knowing what is taking place and why. To be struck down with an illness or accident is, of course, bad enough, and many people will seek in vain for answers to the questions 'Why did this happen to me, why precisely me; what meaning, what justice is there to this?' In such cases, there are no particular persons the questions can be addressed to, no one who can give a definitive answer, since there is no particular person who has *wished* – and thereby caused – what has happened to me. In cases where the pain involved is a result of one person's actions or several people's the questions the outraged person seeks an answer to are partly simpler and partly more complex. The matter may seem to be simpler in those cases where my pain is assumed to be precisely what the other person wished to inflict on me: as a victim I have not been hit 'at random', on the contrary, I have been deliberately singled out by the person behind the abuse. But why have I been so? That there is a person the question can be asked of does not necessarily mean that a meaningful answer can be obtained. An assailant only knows perhaps that he has wished to harm precisely me and may be lost for an answer as to why that wish originated.

The phenomenon we are addressing here can be called the *transportation of psychic pain.* When person A transports some of his psychic pain onto person B, this is something that can take place in a host of different ways, between the two following extremes: as a one-off occurrence or as something daily and lasting; as something both parties, or just the one, or neither of them are aware of; as something both, or only one, or neither of them can give an account of and articulate plausible reasons for. What is it that is transported, to be more precise?

We have a need of getting rid of what is experienced as painful. One way of doing this is to pass what is painful on to someone else, someone who is susceptible to it. The aim is alleviation, relief. To shift something painful onto someone else is not the same as wanting to *share* the pain with someone else. The shifting has more the nature of a relocation: out of me and over onto you, so that what is moved leaves me and is absorbed by you. You bear it *instead of* my doing so. For *someone* has got to bear the pain. It can be noted that this, from a psychological (as well as moral) point of view, is a primitive, even infantile, way of considering the problem of human pain. Even if it can – indeed, ought – to be replaced by a more mature way of looking at things, we cannot omit mentioning its status as completely fundamental for all of us.

I can – to explore this view further – attempt to remedy my helplessness by causing someone else to feel helpless; my self-disgust by humiliating someone else; my loss of control by controlling someone else; my fear by making someone else afraid. Only someone who is just as susceptible to, and thus vulnerable to, what is felt to be painful to bear as I myself am will be suitable as an object for my relocation; a thinglike object will not do. It is in this way that pain, in all its various mental qualities, is exchanged between people. To enjoy and relish that the victim has been struck down by pain, that he is abused, loses self-respect and loses his foothold in life calls for such strong terms as evil and sadism. And when such a mode of behaviour is part of an enduring pattern in a person's actions towards others, we talk of *psychopathy*. The psychopath is someone who exploits his social intelligence, his ability to perceive (cognitively) how other people are feeling, what it is they fear and hope for, can tolerate and cannot tolerate, as a weapon in his efforts to hurt people at their very weakest spots, so that the pain is as great as possible. To cause impotence and helplessness, in extreme cases even self-abandonment, in another person can give the person committing the outrage a feeling of omnipotence. And with this experienced – or rather imagined – omnipotence comes the illusion of having made oneself invulnerable: it is *the others* who are vulnerable, who are clearly hurt and lack the power to strike back, in short: those who via their eminent vulnerability 'demonstrate' that they only exist to be hurt. Particularly self-centred individuals will only experience other people as an extension of themselves, as mere means to their own ends, and thus devoid of independent wishes, wills and needs, with the limits and the respect that the recognition of such separateness *ought* to give rise to.

The mode of thought in individuals who most clearly display such traits of behaviour has been described as follows: 'To rely on is to need; to need is to be vulnerable; to be vulnerable is to be hurt; and to be hurt is once more to experience the utmost and desperate helplessness of a little child that is deprived of its feeling of greatness.'[15] Even though this description, made by psychiatrist Otto Kernberg, was meant for psychopaths, it contains a core of truth that I would claim is universally human. It is an important point for me that we avoid pathologizing the phenomenon *the transportation of psychic pain*, even though psychiatrists may be right that psychopaths – individuals with serious and morbid narcissism (self-centredness) and an inability to see and respect the needs and limits of *others* – are to be considered the most active and above all *dangerous* transporters – inflictors and locators – of such pain. What we see fully developed in the psychopath are traits all of us can – and ought to be able – to recognize in ourselves: a tendency to be self-centred, to give our own needs a higher priority that those of others, and thus to consider and treat others, especially those who seem to be particularly weak and vulnerable, as means rather than as ends in themselves; to compensate for our own vulnerability by dominating others; to conceal uncertainty behind a mask of certainty; to glorify what is strong and tough, and the demonstrated ability to tolerate quite a lot of it without becoming 'soft'.

The psychotherapist Eva Tryti writes that she, on the basis of many years' clinical experience, finds that 'evil acts are a very important cause of mental afflictions'.[16] At the same time she is worried that the insight into the extent to which mental afflictions would seem to be interpersonally created is not taken sufficiently seriously. Both in the public health sector and the predominant organization of treatment, in public debate and the leading professional approach, it is at present factors *within* the individual that are seen as the cause of mental afflictions, especially biological and genetic causes. One of Tryti's important points is that as the *intrapersonal* approach – and thus the individual-centred treatment – becomes increasingly universal, people are losing sight of the extent to which pain, always individually lived and suffered, has its origins in circumstances and persons *outside* the sufferer himself. The everyday and in many ways subtle, indirect and invisible infliction of pain by one person on another thus also remains hidden. When the *interpersonal* dynamics are not focused on, a playing down of the origins of pain in acts by others takes place, which in the final resort turns the professional aid apparatus with all its experts into loyal allies of those responsible.

To downplay pain inflicted on the other person, or to deny that it has taken place at all, is the favourite strategy of all kinds of inflictors of pain, and not restricted in any way to offenders that psychiatry would term psychopaths. It manifests itself as a conception that the abused person has deserved it. Unfortunately, this way of perceiving and describing the person is often taken over by the person himself, as a confirmation of the abuser's picture of reality. If nothing else, the self-rebuking and self-despising provides a certain 'meaning' for what takes place: to get what one deserves can be said to have a certain logic, possibly even a kind of moral. In a way, the world is left intact – it was only oneself who was at fault, and now the balance has been re-established. If this mode of thought, launched by the abuser, confirmed by the outside world and internalized by the injured party, is taken to its extreme, the abuser may even seem to be someone who has acted in the service of good rather than evil.

No matter how perverted such an interpretation might seem to be, it does suggest a certain order, a certain predictability between cause and effect, the sinner and the punishment, the psychological importance of which for the abused party should not be underestimated. The premise is that not finding any meaning can make a person ill; this is the *clinical* sense in which humans are meaning-dependent and so meaning-craving beings. When the truth about the abuse and the abuser is forbidden, is linked to the destruction of the world, to losing everything and everyone, to getting everyone against one because one knows one will not be believed, since the truth is so painful for all those involved and any other (i.e.

untrue) interpretation is to be preferred, and feels less shameful, then even the abused person can end up supporting the abuser's version. In such abuses as incest and paedophilia, where the most forbidden and outrageous acts have taken place, in an absolute breach of trust and security, of the adult's responsible and loving care for the vulnerable child, the abused party can easily become – and always remain – a victim in the (interpretative) sense in addition to the physical sense. To risk experiencing that no one will believe one as one is defying the taboos and speaking out can be so painful, so lonely and hopeless that it affects the mind. It becomes an abuse on top of the original one, a second rejection. The abused person starts to doubt: since nobody will confirm what has been experienced, seen, heard, smelled, done as being identical with what is most forbidden, secret and unutterable, it has perhaps not happened, it is perhaps simply something I am imagining. Mental reality does not thrive when completely on its own, as the reality of just *one* person, as incapable of being shared with and confirmed by someone else, a living soul somewhere, sometime. The mental reality of *one* subject needs an anchorage in the world outside its inner space, needs confirmation as can only be provided by *intersubjectivity*. The person who remains unseen and that which remains overlooked do not *exist*. Other people are needed to lend validity to what has been experienced, to make it *feel* real. This goes for all persons, in all phases of life, not only childhood.

That this is so may appear mind-boggling and downright irrational. It is a profound fact about human existence nonetheless: it is better to have a meaning that causes pain, that presents one as 'deserving' even what is most painful, than to have no meaning at all. For when meaning exists, or rather is established and maintained by the person involved, the possibility is created for a reconciliation with what has happened.

To blame the victim is not only tempting for the person who abuses others, but also for outsiders. If nothing serious has taken place, nothing that is wrong, one does not need an outsider to intervene. One does not need to expose oneself to the anger and resistance of the abuser, to quarrel with a person who has already shown himself to be ruthless. By excluding the recognition of others' infliction of pain on yet others, one avoids having to accept all the discomfort that accompanies the insight into what humans can do to each other, including oneself. The cost of this denial of reality is furthermore paid for by the weaker party, the one unable to offer resistance (in the short term, it should be noted, not in the long term).

The list is long of the costs of playing down and explaining away the interpersonal – characterized by interaction – element of psychic pain, the fact that pain does not at all have to *originate from* its present bearer here and now. As the famous Swiss psychologist Alice Miller has argued in a number of books, victims often become perpetrators.[17] The pain B was inflicted by A, and is passed on to C who, unable to directly retaliate, will in turn pass it on to D. And so on, in one long chain of person-to-person transported pain. Miller's pithy formulation is: 'Every abuser has once been a victim of abuse', and she takes the traumatic childhoods of a number of well-known people as empirical material, including that of Adolf Hitler. Along with most specialists I feel that Miller's formulation is a considerable exaggeration, and that there are abusers that are genuine 'first movers', i.e. the starting point for the above chain reaction. Nevertheless, Miller succeeds in directing our attention towards an indisputable phenomenon, the need to get rid of something that feels unbearable by sending it away, by directing it at certain other people, although these are often 'selected' for random reasons. She thus draws our attention to the importance of breaking the evil circle of pain transportation.

The picture that Miller paints needs to be supplemented. As she herself has discussed in some of her books, being given a function as an object and 'container' for another person's psychic pain can lead to a wide range of different reactions, not only depending on the nature of the abuse and the pattern of the interaction between the parties but also on the personality of the person assigned such a role. In adult–child relationships characterized by 'reverse parenting', where the child from an early age learns to be considerate towards a mother or father who gives the impression of being extremely fragile, of possibly falling to pieces as a result of the most minor error or lack of attentiveness, a child that is particularly sensitive will gradually develop a form of super-sensitivity, an incredibly finely meshed ability to pick up the fragile adult's mood and needs in a broad mental and affective sense. The child will always have the task of being able to take a hint, of being on the spot to give the desired refill, to be affected by the adult's affectedness. And guess what? Quite often, these super-empathetic, ever-attentive children end up as therapists in their professional adult life, in a lifelong practising of the role of caring and refilling that they have learned in their early childhood, and that in certain cases takes root – is internalized – as the only possible and conceivable 'script' for the person's way of living and acting, the only role he or she will ever become familiar with. To be made invisible regarding one's *own* needs, wishes and projects as a child, so that the will and ability to *have* anything like that of one's own – and to have the courage to communicate it to other people, and possibly even to *demand* something of other people – have been neglected and have lain fallow from the outset, can just as easily lead to an adult life characterized by the continued practising of the self-effacing *giver* role as to a change of roles of the kind Miller originally postulated, where one fine day the cowed child, now an adult, will do to others what others had first done to it – assuming the opportunity presents itself and children or other particularly vulnerable people are available for passing on the pain.

Against this background, it is understandable that therapists say that the most important thing they work on in their therapy with many patients is to stimulate the emergence of a 'healthy egoism'. The patients are not self-assertive enough, they demand too little on their own behalf – not too much or everything, as do psychopaths. Some of these patients, whose afflictions have to do with the feeling of insufficiency, emptiness and apathy, with cooped-up rage whose origins are unknown and which they are scared to lift the lid on, are perhaps victims of the type of mental abuses Miller depicts with consummate skill. When pain is located in a defenceless and uncomprehending child, when an adult attacks imagined and asserted errors and shortcomings in the child as a result of having split off precisely these characteristics from themselves (by what, following psychoanalyst Melanie Klein, is called 'projective identification')[18] the boundaries between the child and the adult are blurred or even extinguished. That which is real, and the meaning that is to be assigned to it, is not something that is established by a mutual exchange between the two; instead, there is something that is completely dictated by the one party, who does not tolerate the slightest reminder that something which has happened is experienced in any other way by others. As the saying has it: when the all-dominant person in the family is cheerful, everybody else is and when he is the opposite, everyone is anxiously watchful, fearing the fits of anger that might be imminent.

The attack on the other person's self, on the other person's positive self-esteem and value, goes hand in hand with the annihilation of the mental reality of the other person, by its being denied any form of validity or value; psychopaths are particularly active as well as harmful in doing this, of course, but it is not their prerogative: the inclination at work is human, all too human. With such a life-story a lot of hard work is needed to rebuild all that has been pulled down for good – work the person is unable to do alone but which requires another person's independent support and confirmation. Since anyone who from an early age has been most familiar with disrespect will tend to meet every giver, every approver, with distrust, we are dealing with an enormous gap that has to be bridged. For anyone who has been abused time after time, the meeting with a person who seems to be good and unselfish can release a strong feeling of ambivalence. It is hard to completely believe that it is true, that one deserves something like this, that something that is really good and that it is a question of being given, not just *taken* (from), will be able to last. The need for that which is good, for another person who both has something good and is willing to give one part of it is immeasurable yet at the same time so fragile and supercharged that the person cannot tackle it. Love is destroyed while it is only just starting, before the relationship has really got going. The wounded person prefers to be the rejecter than to risk rejection; prefers appearing as the active party so as to conceal a deep sense of being impotent and unworthy. This is how a self-destructive pattern is confirmed at the very moment the possibility of breaking it was there, of experiencing that one is wrong, that others *can* be good and that one's own goodness *can* be valued rather than exploited or denied or ridiculed. As Freud was so good at pointing out, terming it our deep-seated compulsion to repetition: we engage in self-fulfilling prophecies even when their content is sinister and their effect nothing but self-destructive, a dead end in every respect; we are even wont to return to and to enact our worst traumas – an inclination so deep it requires years on the couch to break free of it and so use one's energies on seeking out what is truly good in life as opposed to what is most painful and spells continued misery.[19]

To return to the main topic: what we need to consider next is the peculiar feeling of *envy,* and the enormous pain it may bring about. That what appears to be genuinely worth admiring in others can give rise to anything but displayed admiration is well known. To ruin the good precisely because it is good, and because one would wish to have it oneself, is the essence of envy, a feeling whose profoundly destructive power within personal relationships is too rarely appreciated in academic psychology and too seldom recognized by those affected in real life.

Envy transports a great deal of psychic pain. To envy someone can be terribly painful, something that motivates one to disguise the feeling as something else. Envy is the other-directed feeling we are least capable of admitting to ourselves and others; it is easier to admit jealousy and greed. Envy is based on my making a comparison between myself and the other person, where the other person comes out as the one who has, does or is exactly what I would most wish I had, did or was, but who I fall pitifully short of in comparison with. I suffer because of this lack. The unbearable thing about the other person consists in his embodying *precisely* what it pains me most that I lack. To meet him is synonymous with being reminded of what I lack, and what I am making every effort to repress. When the repression is no longer possible, I can try another defensive move. I can develop an interpretation where what the other person represents is worth nothing at all. When admiration causes pain, because the admired person merely makes my own shortcomings visible, I can invalidate the admiration by declaring it without an object: what the other person stands for is in actual fact worthless, ignoble, disgusting. Possibly, the other person *imagines* and pretends to be superior to the rest of us; he believes he is something really special, and either he is special (it is just that the special – correctly understood – is negative, not positive) or he is not special at all, and must be punished for his deceit. No matter what the other person does – is proud of himself, gives up everything that is his, or

84

begins to run it down – he cannot win. By attacking it, by physically removing it from this world, by combating it symbolically by denying it any form of quality or validity, the envious person can seek to solve the problem created by envy's gnawing pain once and for all. This is done most effectively where the person or persons who are the subject of envy are forced to take over the assailant's running down of them, i.e. in a Nietzschian 'reassessment of all values' expressed by the best qualities of the envied persons – their goodness, or wisdom, or creative ability – being transformed into their diametric opposite, i.e. to the utterly 'negative' characteristics that will now justify their fall and destruction. What started out as psychologically worth admiring *for* the person who was roused to envy ends up with a quasi-objective and pseudo-moral stamp as valueless *in itself*.

Have we, then, now uncovered the nucleus of psychic pain? Have we answered the question of what comprises its essence? What its deepest sources are?

The Norwegian psychiatrist Svein Haugsgjerd poses the same questions, and answers that by psychic pain he is referring to what Jacques Lacan calls 'lack', or what the British psychoanalyst Wilfred Bion, using an expression from Freud, calls 'caesura', a sudden transition from one state to another, i.e. trauma.[20] Desire, urges and violence are, according to Lacan, cultivated forms deriving from the fact that lack and transience are given conditions of human life, while anxiety and mental conflict are to be seen as more complex effects of the mentioned fundamental elements. We cannot experience the lack as such; it is beyond consciousness. What we can experience, and which motivates our behaviour, is only the above-mentioned derived forms of the lack, according to Lacan's theory. The psychic pain that is generated by the fact that we exist in a state of lack, that we are lacking beings, that we thus live in the absence of fullness of being and perfection, does not, therefore, have to be experienced by the subject *as* pain, but it is, however, always accompanied by pain in relation to, and in the exchange with, other human beings. In that sense, all such person-to-person relations and communications are arenas for the transportation (shifting) of psychic pain. The fact that such pain *is* transportable at all, that it *allows itself* to be shifted, is because we assume that others are lacking beings – beings existing *qua* lack, as it were – like ourselves, sensitive to pain like ourselves.

Is then the transportation of pain, so to speak, the only thing going on, the only way we can try to tackle our own lacking being and exposure to pain? Of course not. We can also, as Haugsgjerd does, talk about the *transformation* of such pain, in the form of a reshaping of the lack from its most basic and primitive forms into the increasingly processed, sophisticated and mature forms. Even though the main contrast involved can seem to be extremely simple and well known, I regard it as so fundamental that I want to make it fully explicit: instead of experiencing the meeting with goodness and ability to provide in other people as something threatening, as triggering off uncertainty, feelings of inferiority and anxiety, it does no harm to show gratitude for something like that existing in this world, and to concrete individuals who are bearers of it. Instead of having one's journey through life coloured by self-centredness and greed, it does no harm to colour it with the joy of giving and with generosity regarding what seem to be different and strange. Instead of fearing that the – large or small amount of – goodness one might possess will be taken away from one as soon as it is displayed, it does no harm to display it confidently in the belief that it will be taken care of and highly valued, not debased and destroyed. Instead of considering others limitlessly good or limitlessly evil, it does no harm to see that others – like oneself – contain both parts, with all the ambivalence that inevitably involves. Instead of denying and repressing one's own aggression and rage, even impulses to attack and one's own fallibility, it does no harm to admit that one actually carries such characteristics around *too*, like everybody else does; thereby the need is diminished for having to project everything painful/evil onto other people, with the subsequent desire to destroy it there, since that is where it is taken to stem from. Instead of denying the damage one has caused others because of such aggression, it does no harm to acknowledge that the damage has been done, that it was one's own fault, so that shown anger can be met with reconciliation in the injured party. The alternatives that I have played off against each other here, and that mark the difference between a primitive and a mature attitude, correspond roughly to the distinction Melanie Klein makes between a schizoid-paranoid and a depressive position.[21]

NINE

The Role of Culture in Dealing with Pain

We have now reached a main theme in any discussion of pain as looked upon in a social perspective: namely that *culture* is of vital importance if individuals are to succeed in taking the step from *transportation* to *transformation* of psychic pain. The key word is *reshaping,* and such reshaping of pain depends on what is called *symbolization,* i.e. the individual is given the chance of processing that which hurts, that generates pain and thus exerts pressure on the inner life of the individual – a pressure that seeks release. Such processing can only take place in a mature and non-destructive way if the individual can make use of various types of symbols from various media. To convert and process psychic pain with the aid of symbolic forms means getting the chance to create images, put words to, give form to the otherwise unbearable inner pressure. This pressure hurts so much and creates such inner tension that it will turn inwards as self-destruction or outwards as destruction aimed at others if it is not released in some *third way* – as words or sounds, images or representations *about* what hurts and creates pain, thus making its underlying sources into something I can relate to as a symbol-using and communicative – i.e. social – being. In this way the 'forms' of these symbols will be experienced as having enough power in them to *bear* (contain) what hurts so much. In other words, the symbolic-indirect relief of everything connected with and felt to be painful, as anxiety-creating and dangerous, must be recognized *and* experienced as a *superior* alternative to concrete-direct relief in the form of trans-portation aimed at others (physical enactment).

By *culture* I shall mean something very specific: the symbolic resources a society places at the disposal of its members, and that every one of them can make use of to tackle everything that makes life painful. While Lacan, as we have seen, places most emphasis on human existence meaning to be in – and suffer under – a state of lack, I place greatest emphasis on it meaning to be placed in this world within a framework of certain non-choosable fundamental conditions, such as dependence, vulnerability, mortality, fragility of relations and existential loneliness. The fundamental conditions are not necessarily the direct causes of experienced pain. Rather, what matters and so needs to be appreciated in some detail is the way the conditions are typically interpreted and evaluated within a given society at a given point in its history, whereby culture is the all-important medium for such symbolic activity. The conditions I am referring to should therefore be seen as what provides an origin and breeding ground for our common exposure to pain, so that it pains us to be maltreated *because* we are fundamentally vulnerable, so that it pains us to be abandoned and alone *because* we are fundamentally dependent, so that serious illness gives rise to anxiety or even depression *because* we are mortal, etc.

If I let my gaze slide along the walls of the Edvard Munch museum I can recognize many of my own existential concerns in the pictures on display. I can immediately see which pictures have to do with fear, sorrow, melancholy and jealousy. There is a great deal of pain in Munch's pictures – created as they probably were out of what was often utterly painful in Munch's own life – such as his sister's illness and early death, or his own bouts of anxiety, bordering on nervous breakdown in certain periods. These biographical facts are – precisely – not the point, however. What is instructive for my argument here is how Munch the artist has managed

89

to *shape* his existential pain in a way that directly addresses me in my pain and you in yours. This is because Munch has something universal as his theme: he is preoccupied with the five fundamental conditions I have just mentioned. By painting so many variations on this limited set of basic themes, Munch presents – archetypally, as it were – some of the various ways a human being can try and deal with them in his own life. What Munch does, then, is partly to use himself and partly to explore and expand a symbolic space in order to express such universal concerns as angst, fear, loneliness, melancholy and jealousy. By our visiting the pictures, entering into their universe, making use of the symbolism in the displayed interaction between the persons, in the contact or estrangement between them, in the ties entered into or broken, cherished or feared, in the two persons' interdependence or loneliness, Munch allows us to process our own experiences. We can open up to the pain we carry round with us, the pain of hoping yet also knowing that we can be disappointed, of daring to love yet also knowing that we can be rejected, of feeling deeply for others yet also knowing that we can be hurt. The pressure within us finds release, made possible by the reshaping force of the symbolization, this being the major alternative to a physical-concrete enactment of the hurt in the form of relocating it in others so as to attack it there – as if everything that creates pain in the world had originally come from these other persons and not from ourselves and the substance of which our own life has been made.

To be sure, to some readers this may seem a highly banal rendition of Munch's art. It is true that his paintings create disquiet for many people rather than calm, that they have a sting in them that can intensify anxiety and depressive thoughts rather than soothe them. In that sense, you may leave the exhibition of his paintings more confused than you were before seeing them, not less. My concern here is the unashamedly humanist one: that great artists – forgers of symbols more than anyone else – lend meaning the expression that 'nothing human is alien to me', not even the greatest anxiety, despair and loneliness. Cultural products of the type that Munch's paintings are examples of can be said from this perspective to be results of the transformation of psychic pain – and to be potential vehicles for such transformation in their onlookers. To watch a film, play or dance can give rise to the same experience, that of entering an artistically created human universe, a space one can enter in order to dwell on as well as marvel at the depths of the human repertoire, at who and what we are, for better or for worse. At best, culture functions as both cause and effect in this respect: culture enables humans to enter and use all the resources for processing and reforming that a particular society's symbolic universe offers, at the same time as the cultural manifestations themselves produced by experiencing the fundamental conditions of existence in general, and psychic pain in particular. As especially Melanie Klein has sought to demonstrate, all transformation processes presuppose that there is not only pain or lack but also a force – fed by the capacity for guilt and remorse – that continually pulls us in the direction of what she calls reparation, understood as the desire to make good again what has been attacked, to heal what has been broken because one was envious of its goodness or was too greedy to share it with others.

This brings us to an important insight. The fact that we are beings exposed to pain, that we live in lack and *as* lack (Lacan) should not be interpreted as meaning that what causes pain is what dominates and will inevitably dominate our lives. Our exposure to pain and our lack as beings admittedly tinge our lives with gravity. But these basic characteristics of our existence certainly do not pull us unambiguously in the direction of dwelling on what causes pain. For to be susceptible to pain means being sensitive and to be sensitive means to be able to experience what is good: to be given what is good by others, in the form of love and care. That is why when sensitivity is worn down, when hardening and numbness replace it, the individual not only avoids the vulnerability of possibly being rejected and insulted but also the joy of being met, seen and accepted when one opens up, exposes oneself in one's vulnerability. The person who for some reason or other is no (longer) capable of being affected, cannot be affected in a *good* way either, in a life-supportive and affirmative way. To encapsulate oneself as a result of self-imposed or dictated hardening risks becoming a strategy for losing affectedness with all that is good in the world, all that makes life worth living. A zest for life and joy, an urge to make contact and the appetite for gaining knowledge and wisdom, curiosity regarding the unknown and untried – all these things *also* derive from the mentioned fundamental conditions. That we are in a state of lack in a basic sense disposes us to want to enrich and expand ourselves through contact with the good in the world, that which others might happen to have in greater measure than ourselves; this provides a basic motivation to protect everything that is good instead of seeking to destroy it. While the transportation of psychic pain is the common denominator of all the ways in which inner lack and pain are enacted, with the maltreatment or ruin of other human beings as a result, the transformation of pain is the alternative and corrective to the transportation of pain. The incentive to affirm and protect the good in the world is just as basic and eradicable as its opposite.

One of the advantages of placing such emphasis on how pain is shifted, how it is located here and there because of social interaction is that the distinctly psychiatric look at the *frozen forms* of human suffering, i.e. the various *states* of suffering, are supplemented by a keen eye for the dynamic processes – the actions – that cause the sufferings.[22] Here, we recall Eva Tryti's words about the vast extent to which mental sufferings are the result of abusive acts by others, of having been forced or manipulated into the role of a bearer of *someone else's* pain. What is suffered subjectively has been brought about and maintained intersubjectively, i.e. interpersonally. Consequently, the wounds can only be healed by trying to change the patterns of interaction that continuously produce and intensify such sufferings. In my opinion, this is not first and foremost to be seen as a task for experts, for professional therapists, for I warn against pathologizing (morbidizing) as well as professionalizing our exposure to pain and ways of dealing with it. No, it is a task for each and every one of us, a task that refers us to culture's accessible symbolic resources – as I allowed Munch's paintings to illustrate.

I have maintained that culture in the sense defined above has an immensely important role to play: culture decides what possibilities we have to deal with our pain in ways that are not dangerous or even directly fatal for others, and ultimately for ourselves, if we do not control our tendency to attack those who are associated with something bad and hurtful, or with something that is so good that our own lack of this goodness causes us to devaluate it and destroy it (the motive force behind envy). Svein Haugsgjerd is maybe overdramatizing a bit – though only a bit – when he says 'the contrast between transportation and transformation of psychic pain' corresponds to 'the contrast between barbarism and culture'.[23]

Now that we have emphasized the role of culture in enabling us as individuals to transform our – and other people's – pain *instead* of moving it by relocating it in other concrete beings, we must ask the question: can our culture, that which characterizes our society today, be said to be carrying out this task, or is culture presently letting us down in this respect?

By placing a reservoir of symbol-transmitted representations of basic human experiences, effects and states of mind at our disposal, a culture offers forms and ways that allow us to adopt an attitude that is not repressive or denying but con-cessive and recognizing to all aspects (including the darkest and most dangerous) of our repertoire as human beings. If culture lets us down in this function, the result can be an enactment of what is prevented in its symbol-utilizing pro-cessing. One way culture can fail is by offering individuals representations and pictures of aggression and destructive-ness that are too concrete, in the sense that the hurtful is imitated and thus in a way repeated within the symbolic medium instead of being given an abstract and thereby processed form. The point is that the richer and more elastic the internalized images of destructiveness are in an individ-ual, the less will the need be to enact the destructive impulse towards other real people. The meaning of culture, therefore, has to do with stimulating the ability to imagine the painful and dangerous aspect of being a human being instead of enacting it: to imagine the hurtful and painful as the alterna-tive – the only one – to actually doing it.

For individuals who lack images for their own destruc-tiveness, it will, in the absence of symbols, be intimately linked to the body. The body then becomes in an over-con-crete way the tool for getting rid of one's urge to hurt, to move the painful out and away, the bodily enactment the result, no matter whether it is turned inwards (self-injury) or outwards. The more impoverished the inner symbolic uni-verse, the shorter the path to bodily action, understood as the externalization of the forces that did not find room and were 'carried' into an inner world of ideas. Admittedly, imagina-tion and creativity are characteristics of the individual person, more developed in some than others. Nonetheless, to be able to imagine and 'make' something in a symbolic form of what must feel difficult within oneself can be seen as abil-ities in the individual that feed on nourishment provided by the symbol-bearing culture outside the individual, and that occupy the space – the in-between area – between the mental inner life of the individual and the outside world. Culture has to do with creating meaning, with allowing individuals to do so, successfully, in their distinct individual ways, always *in situ* and for their own purposes, a meaning that different persons utilize in their highly individual ways, depending on the experiences they make and the resources they bring to the encounter with them. *Symbols* indicate here that something relatively abstract stands for (represents) something concrete, something that actually exists, just as Munch's pictures of and about anxiety give me an image of *my* anxiety, a picture of *my* jealousy towards *that* person, etc. From a psychological point of view, the formation of symbols has to do with the child's need to protect its – both loved and hated – objects (i.e. mother, father, who the child is abandoned to and dependent on and that it can therefore feel rage towards as well as gratitude) from the effects of its attacks. The symbol is needed in order to shift aggression from the original concrete object (mother, father), so that the feeling of guilt is alleviated to the extent the object avoids aggression.[24] Aggression can now be enacted in a mental universe, towards *substitutes* for its real objects in the physical world – substitutes that can be precisely that since they have been given a symbolic form. Accordingly there is an element of *moving* also in what we formerly referred to as the transformation (processing, reshaping) of psychic pain. More precisely, the alternatives have either to do with the experienced and suffered pain being shifted onto other actual people so as to be combated and attacked there, with any damage that might cause, or the actually experienced pain being shifted from its original concrete objects (aims) onto a symbolic substitute, where it is subsequently 'taken out' within the symbol-using space – that of culture.

The idea is not that the urge to destroy completely will cease to be a basic aspect of the individual psyche. The idea is that culture allows the urge – uneradicable as it is – to remain within a world of fantasy and imagination or, to put it another way, to remain an imagined potentiality instead of an enacted actuality. It is important to realize that my message is not that the individual's aggression and desire to destroy is to be suppressed, locked in. On the contrary, what really threatens society is precisely the suppression and denial of individuals' personal aggression. Why?

In their famous work *The Dialectic of Enlightenment*, Frankfurt School philosophers Max Horkheimer and Theodor Adorno have given the following answer to the question I posed above concerning the state of culture in our present-day society.[25] They contend that the control that modern man has gained over outside nature plays no role in the attainment of freedom and happiness unless man has learnt how to control himself, i.e. his own destructiveness as a source of disorder, unhappiness and cruelty. This does not mean that one's inner nature only is dangerous and only has to be controlled. Not at all. Too much self-control and too strong renunciation – an inner regime characterised by zero tolerance – regarding every spontaneous instinctual urge can create individuals who are 'on the lookout' for opportunities to *finally* find an outlet for all that is shut in and forbidden – opportunities promised by ideologies which praise violence and violent practices – with total freedom of action for a physical enactment of everything that is hurtful. What is decisive, then, is to reach a self-knowledge, a self-composure as regards the equal potential of the inner nature to want evil as much as good – something which, according to Melanie Klein, gives rise to a deep-seated fear in humans of infecting the good with the bad, of spoiling love with hate – in short, of being unfortunate enough to ruin everything that is dearest to us.[26] Such self-knowledge – of being the source of both good and evil and *which is which* – will lessen the need in the individual person to project his own inner conflicts onto others (Klein's projective identification) and to attack and defeat them there. The most violent – potentially violence-creating – effects and sources of unrest are inside us; we are driven by them, and we need to put up with the fact that we are driven in this way, by inner forces we have not chosen to be there but that we, even so, depending on the maturity of the afore-mentioned self-composure, have a responsibility to decide what attitude we should adopt towards.

TEN

Pain and Evil

At this juncture we cannot avoid confronting the relevance of evil for our theme of pain and what we do with it. Evil – or sadism for that matter (which is not identical with evil but an important aspect of it) – is naturally not a new theme for us, not least because we discussed torture earlier. In the following discussion, however, the perspective is a different one. The relevance of evil for my insistence on the connection between pain and the fundamental conditions of life consists in the fact that evil, to quote the American philosopher C. Fred Alford, 'is what reveals to us the limits of what it means to be human'.[27] The desire to do that which is bad, to wish to inflict suffering, has got to do with evil transcending boundaries. Let us look at this in more detail.

As I have only hinted at so far, the accepted and often repeated assertion that pain is something humans hate and seek to avoid is only half the truth about the human attitude to pain. The other half has to do with how we seek it, intensify it, create it and are fascinated by it – whether it be our own pain (difficult to understand) or that of others (easier to understand). As will gradually become clear, pain has a great deal to do with limits: with limits being given, being met with, and with how we – as a culture and as individuals – react as regards limits. Limits represent a challenge. Limits in the sense in which we are dealing with them here are something we are faced with, something we are forced to tackle. How do we do so? The two main alternatives are that we either respect limits and treat them as untouchable and unalterable, that we adjust to them, adapt to them or that we do everything in our power – both as a culture and as individuals – to defy them, change them, move or remove them, in so many different attempts to manipulate and control them for our own purposes.

Evil has to do with the willed causing of suffering in another person and against that person's will. I said that evil takes the form of a transcending of limits. The question is: why is such a transcendence something we are driven towards? I think there are a number of valid answers, and that evil is a good way into an important partial answer. C. Fred Alford writes that 'limits are just as frightening as their absence, because they tell us that we are human, subject to constraint, isolation, contingency, morality and death. Everything we are, everything we will become, precludes our being and becoming a thousand other things.'[28] To do something evil to a real, as opposed to an imagined, object is to defy the given limits, to cross them out: to kill is to make oneself a master over life and death, to experience – if only for an instant – omnipotence, to be invulnerable, immortal, autonomous. It is to make demands on existence's element of vitality, or force and life, as its only element, and thereby deny that existence is 'only had', that life is only lived, as *both parts*: as vitality and death, where the one cannot have any meaning without the contrast – and so endured cohabitation – of its opposite.

Alford links evil to sadism. Our theme is not evil as such, with all its possible causes, forms and effects. I will refer to Alford's analysis because it sheds light on certain aspects of pain that we have not yet looked at. Sadism is used here as a term for a person's active attempt to create and control suffering (pain) in others, instead of – as the sadist's only conceived alternative – experiencing the suffering himself. For the sadist there is – broadly speaking – only an either-or solution: me or the others. The underlying logic is that all pain that I do not inflict on or relocate in others I will have to bear myself. In short, the sadist deals with his own pain by shifting it onto something (someone) outside himself rather than processing it, in the form of a sequence in the outside world, not a reshaping with the aid of symbols in the inner world, in the form of using (misusing) others in the service of relieving pain. Sadism is taking matters – the pain – into one's own hands, quite literally. It is to actively carry out something with it, in order to remove the burden of it, i.e. in the form of pushing it away from oneself over onto others – as if pain was a physical, transportable thing in the world, some sort of object (read: person) that can be controlled (planted, intensified) in the other person by shifting it away from oneself.

The sadist acts on the assumption that the only way the pain of being human and thereby in a state of lack, of not being perfect, can be dealt with is by involving some other living person in it. If this is to work, the sadist must assume that the other person is just as vulnerable as he is himself. We have to realise that sadism is *not* a question of dehumanization, of blankly denying the other person's (co-)humanity; on the contrary, it is a project that crucially relies on perceiving the other person as just as suitable for suffering as oneself, i.e. as equally vulnerable and sensitive to pain. Alford remarks that we now can see why sadism is most accurately referred to as sadomasochism – it is the *identification* of the person with his chosen human victim that is the core of the action; without that there would be no point to it.[29] *Things* in the physical world are not considered suitable for the relocation of pain; only what is alive and exposed to pain *as* one is oneself can offer the prospect of being able to take in and house the pain and the discomfort that burns inside one and is felt to be intolerable. Pain in this sense can only (be attempted to) be moved around in those similarly disposed, in beings whose exposure to it and discomfort at it are basically identical.

From this perspective the difference between sadism and sadomasochism is small, the transition almost imperceptible. However, the aim of the sadomasochist is not quite the same as that of the sadist, i.e. one's own pleasure deriving from the generation of pain in others – it is in fact far more radical. The aim of the infliction of pain is deeper than the psychological motive that lies in the legendary sneer at the victim's screams of pain, pleasure at the discomfort caused – mental as well as physical – in the other. The aim is profound – to destroy reality, i.e. the reality of difference and individuality, the fact that the other person is *also* different, not just like me. The completely intolerable is not restricted to the non-chosen fact that consists in having been born into a world as dependent, vulnerable and moral, and thereby as exposed to the experience of pain that are the inevitable result of such conditions (in addition to the ways in which they enable joy, contact and recognition, as we saw above). It can also be felt as intolerable that others have different ways of tackling these universally human conditions, or that some people evidently imagine that they are above pain, above immanence; that they believe themselves better than I, I who have feared it as the worst of all discomforts. Those who seek to *transcend* pain, make it marginal instead of experiencing it as fundamental, I will reach via my targeted infliction of pain, pull them down from such an arrogant delusion; down to my level, reminding them that precisely at this basic level we are similar rather than dissimilar, fellow human beings rather than unique individuals. When pain catches up with each and every one, high and low, it also brings about impressive *levelling* within the social area. Pain unites, creates equality where there were differences, forces even the seriously thinking person to abandon all energy and projects related to transcendence, going beyond the body – or denial – that we first and foremost are animal beings, imprisoned in our physical nature as the scene of intolerable infliction of pain. To link back to the section on torture with which I began the book, the sadistic element in torture seems to extort a self-abandonment out of the other person, an abandonment initially of the person's values here in life, and ultimately – when the pain is so overwhelming that all vitality ebbs away – a rejection of the actual value of life, i.e. a of the wish to go on living. This is the total victory – if such an expression can be used – that the sadist can seek to achieve: that the victim is induced to hate himself, to hate his existence and to curse the day he was born – that not to live is preferred to going on living.

It is here that sadism as a project can be said to enter into a particularly strong and dangerous alliance with envy. As we know from many sources, not least literary ones (Claggart who hates the eponymous character in Melville's novel *Billy Budd*, for example), it is in particular the virtuous, splendid and fine that are the subject of envy and that are sought to be destroyed, which means that these qualities acknowledged as being positive – and that others precisely feel they lack – are exposed to violent attacks, verbally and mentally as well as physically. The sadist views the pain of others as an aim in itself, so that pain, as well as actually creating it oneself, give rise to joy. Envy, in the strong variant we are dealing with here, expresses itself as the felt pain at certain others appearing to be happy or good; pain born of others' happiness can only be transformed into a situation full of one's own happiness if the other person is no longer able to feel any happiness, but only pain instead. Other ways of dealing with one's own unhappiness (lack) in the light of others' happiness are not recognized.[30]

While the project of overcoming having to suffer oneself, the sensitivity to pain, is undoubtedly a characteristic of many aggressors, it is just as important to look at the experience of relief (even if only for a brief respite) experienced by causing and witnessing suffering in another person only actually being possible if the aggressor admits to himself that he 'knows' what it feels like to suffer in the way the other person is now doing. He knows this because he is a human being like the other person; and he has to let the other person remain a human being like himself if the identification at issue here is to be retained. Indeed, there are reasons for claiming that the sadist acknowledges the reality of suffering in human life to such an extent that he is tempted to idealize it – by considering the ability to withstand suffering a sign of inner strength, as Alford believes Nietzsche tends towards on several occasions, and as we – to change from a philosopher to a practician and organizer – recall that Reichsführer-SS Heinrich Himmler advocated in his speeches to the officers who were responsible for the systematic killing done at the extermination camps:

> We all know what it means when 100 dead women and children lie there, or when 1000 do so. Even so, I think I can say that this – the most difficult order we have been issued so far – was executed without allowing our men to suffer any damage in mind or in spirit. The danger was very real: the line between the two potentials – to become cruel and heartless and to lose respect for human life, or else to turn soft and break down – is incredibly fine. To have persisted and at the same time to have remained decent men … this is a page of glory in our history that has never been written and is never to be written.[31]

We must recognize that the step from idealizing one's own suffering to idealizing inflicting it on others is short, especially if withstanding pain is glorified as a sign of strength, as the great test of character in life and 'the struggle', so that the way one reacts when encountering intense pain is seen as revealing more than anything else who one is, what stuff one is made of. From historical examples – with the extermination of the Jews by the Nazis as a climax so far – we know that *hardening*, in the form of targeted 'exercises' to tolerate a great deal of pain, ever more pain, without noticing it, functions as a preparatory manoeuvre and thereby a condition for later being able to inflict the greatest suffering on the selected victims without being affected by it. To stay hard in situations where it would be easy to become soft, to be able to continue when to stop would possibly seem to be an immense liberation – *that* is what the test of character is about, a test that only 'the very best' (Himmler) will pass. The (illusory) final result of such hardening processes is to consider oneself as beyond the reach of pain, as so 'hard' that sensitivity to pain has been overcome.

The corrective to this perversion of the essence of one's moral nature is not only a question of learning to accept that one will come to suffer and inevitably come to inflict suffering on others in the course of one's life, since life and pain are two sides of the same coin (as Nietzsche points out). No, the important thing is to regret that it is so, to regret it while holding onto the insight that it is so. In short, Nietzsche's idealization of the reality of suffering has to be supplemented with Melanie Klein's insights if it is not to become dangerous – with Klein's emphasis on *reparation*, that is to say, on one's ability to wish to put right the damage one has caused.

We need, however, to go beyond an intrapsychic perspective as well as a dyadic (I–you) one in order to recognize the importance of culture in teaching individuals good rather than damaging ways of dealing with the peculiar pressure that is formed inside one as a result of unbearable pain creating fear and a pressure towards shifting everything hurtful onto other people. Culture understood as a public space in a wide, symbol-transmitted sense shows – holds up to individuals – that aggression and fear have other places to go, to be tackled and processed, than the concrete place constituted by the physical meeting between two people. In creativity that unfolds and is stimulated in the cultural space, 'a voice is given the creature for its woe',[32] a voice to live with the pain of existence, instead of placing pain out alive by causing it in real persons. Understood in this way, culture is itself psyche. Via cycles of projective identification with gods and other cultural ideals and artefacts and the subsequent reintrojection of these (that they are once more taken 'into' individuals) a given culture starts to acquire the form of a psyche, albeit in an exaggerated or distorted way. This does not mean that culture lives its own life, that it acts as a group self. As Alford points out: 'Cultural forces are psychological forces; they become so via projection and introjection. As a psychological defence, culture will reflect many of the most intense mental conflicts and defences to its members.'[33] What makes the tragedians of antiquity such discerning psychologists is the way in which they depict *external* conflicts in such a way that they can represent – give *a shape* to and offer images and representations about – *internal* ones. Fairytales and myths still have the same function. At the level of culture, inner conflicts and effects *must* be given a symbolic form in an outer – in the sense of publicly accessible – medium. The point is that we acknowledge the fact that what is symbolized in something external is *not* external, does not originate in something or someone outside us, but in something internal.

How are we to understand the task of culture more closely? When we can say that culture is successful – or possibly unsuccessful – in forming our attitude and strategies regarding the reality of pain?

Expressed positively, what a culture is able to do is to offer individuals symbolic resources in a wide sense so that they can manage to acknowledge the most unpleasant thing of all: that pain follows human life from birth to death, that pain is always and for everyone a present possibility, if not an experienced reality, and that an all-too-human way of reacting to the discomfort this gives rise to is to seek (consciously or unconsciously) to shift pain away from oneself onto others, to turn something internal into something external. Freud talked about 'the culture and its discontents' (*Das Unbehagen in der Kultur*); here we are looking at the potential that exists in culture as a symbolic relief for discomfort in the individual. Culture can allow me to extract, feel, dwell on whatever creates discomfort in me, by offering symbolic *substitutes* (representations) of what is hurtful, so that these become my objects, what bears the brunt in my way of handling the painfulness of existence. The child who is angry with his mother bashes his teddy bear and mother escapes. The teddy bear is a 'transitional object' (to make use of psychoanalyst Donald Winnicott's concept); it naturally has a physical existence – which means that in a non-reparable way it can get broken – but psychologically it is its function as a symbol – as the imagined 'stand-in' for mother, the real object of the child's rage – we are dealing with here. When we grow up and hopefully become more mature, the same need to 'extract' inner pain and inner conflicts will assume increasingly less physical, increasingly more abstract forms. Now dwelling on figures, states and mood that remind me of the real objects (persons) or events (traumas) in my life that exert pressure in the form of discomfort and psychic pain inside me, can help me to gain greater clarity as to what the discomfort is about, so that patients in successful psychotherapy declare that 'just putting difficult things into words to somebody else, giving pain a form in a common space and a common language, helped – by taking something of the danger and intensity out of pain'. To *share* within a common space, with the aid of language or images or representations, offers relief, takes away something of what had felt so heavy to carry alone, and thus makes the need to force pain out onto others, to locate it in them and only them, less urgent.

Although I would add – so as not to paint a rosy picture of the healing potential of conversation regarding the individual's psychic pain – that our existential loneliness (one of the five fundamental conditions I have introduced) marks a boundary vis-à-vis others and what others are at all *able* or willing to share with me, *about* me. As the Norwegian poet Halldis Moren Vesaas aptly puts it in a poem: even in the closest relationship, in the lifelong love between two, two that achieve the greatest intimacy with each other – even there the other person will not be able to get behind 'the innermost gate', that which for ever marks off *me* and my inner universe as opposed to *you* and yours. Both sides are true: the fundamental conditions condemn us to an unalleviable loneliness in this existential sense, while language, images, narrative and fantasies as the culture of which we are members offer us the chance of transcending our loneliness, of sharing *something*, although never everything, of what we carry with us in our inner world.

ELEVEN

When Pain is Imitated and Enacted: Violence in Culture

I would argue that the prevailing culture in present-day society is failing in its task as described here. Today, cultural criticism is, in certain circles at any rate, the most unoriginal and least daring exercise that could be imagined. The sort of criticism I would like to promote here, however, is not of the general kind. Rather, it is directed at particular characteristics of the present age, characteristics on which the topic of pain and attitudes to pain is particularly well suited to shed light. Let me explain.

One of the main reasons for culture failing the task we have described is that much of what is presented in the symbol-using public space is too similar *to* the hurtful and evil as enacted in a physical-concrete manner. By too much resembling the originals, i.e. that for which the individual needs relief, these representations cannot succeed in their alleviative and stand-in functions. The images, metaphors, narratives on offer are too imitative – too little abstract, *too little symbolical* in a psychological sense – in relation to the impulses and affects that need to be processed (transformed) in ways that lessen the pressure towards enactment regarding real, as opposed to imagined, objects or persons. Examples include the fact that the vampire – especially in American popular culture – is now in the film industry and many genres the image of evil, instead of Satan, who is of course only meaningful as a contrast to and in a constant struggle with the Good, i.e. within a universe where good and evil are equally real forces: a typical example of how culture promotes rather than prevents the path from impulse to action. The implicit message in fictions where an evil misdoer takes over all control and where the good is conspicuous by its artistic absence is that vulnerability and dependency appear to the onlooker, listener or reader as *even more dangerous*, even more undesirable and sinister than before – with the possible result that attempts to rid oneself of the undesired qualities in oneself become more dramatic and direct, the effects increasingly destructive and directly life-threatening. The end-result of such a trend is films of violence that function quite simply as user manuals.

How does reality TV fit in here? I am no expert in this genre and will restrict myself to a few selective comments. One feature of the changes in the upbringing of children and young people that German researchers in particular have written about is that so-called secondary experiences are increasingly taking over and marginalizing primary experiences.[34] What is meant by this? Not all that long ago, it was usual for young people who went to bed with each other for the first time, who were debutants in a profound sense, not to know all that much, let alone the details, of what happened in sexual intercourse *before* they tried it out for themselves, i.e. as a primary experience. Likewise, a great many emotional, psychological and social phenomena had to wait for their own experience for the person to gain precise ideas about them and what they involved. The primary experience had undisputed pride of place: one's own debut provided the input for a new and until then unknown world. Today, the balance of power is the opposite: it is the secondary experiences – in the form of disseminated knowledge about *other people's* experiences and representations of phenomena that are talked about – that have pride of place; they steal a march on the primary experiences. The result is that the debutant in his own life has a long-standing career behind him as a reader of magazines with representations that are erotically/ pornographically explicit, as a viewer of TV programmes, films, videos, games and DVDs, as a surfer on the Internet of sites with this type of content, etc. Obviously, one's own debut will still mean breaking new ground but not with the same breadth and depth as before, and with the added difference that what one experiences firsthand has precise, detailed and in every respect 'strong' precedents, models and expectations to live up to (just think how teenage magazines of the most widely read kind have changed in the course of a few years to containing ever more detailed and realistic accounts of 'everything about sex': every possible position, technique, 'preference', etc. – a kind of user's manual for the young and perhaps still (primarily) inexperienced readers). This means that the primary experience can easily run the risk of becoming a pale copy, with the secondary as the original, instead of vice versa.

Arguably, in the concept of reality TV this reversal of the original balance of power between the primary and the secondary has been acted out more fully than in any other popular genre. So far we know little about the consequences for the viewers, especially the youngest. In accordance with the inner logic that is given a free rein here and that therefore does not encounter any other limits than those that it possibly creates itself in the process (and what are they, if there are any?), the trend is for increasingly daring, or strong, or provocative and spectacular concepts to be developed to continually replace the old ones, which quickly pale (lose their provocative, not to say sensational power) and appear boring. In philosophical terms we could say, invoking the Danish philosopher Knud E. Løgstrup's concept, that what previously constituted and demarcated the *zone of inviolability* around the individual human being, a protective space around its innermost sphere of modesty, shyness and potential ashamedness, is now gradually being annulled as such a space: instead of being that which a representation (e.g. on TV) avoids, it has become what is zoomed in on, the actual centre, the focal point of the actual course of events, what we as viewers are invited to look straight at.

That these series are quickly developing into concentrating on the lowest common denominator of our age, in the form of sex, violence and various excesses and barrier-breaking activities in a combination of the above, comes as no surprise. Here voyeuristic viewers can at close quarters dwell on precisely the phenomena and acts that the art and culture of earlier epochs were content merely to suggest, and then in the form of fiction, unlike now in the form of filming/monitoring real actions carried out – in the tremendously effective here-and-now of direct transmission, provided by omnipresent, never-resting cameras – *by real people*, people who are not 'playing the part of' someone else but who are themselves in everything they do. Here, someone's primary experiences are the secondary experiences of the many: the viewers. It is just that, unlike fiction and thereby the classic artistic-symbolic expressions/representations, the actor-participants of the reality series neither represent nor imitate nor suggest the actions we are dealing with: they quite simply *perform* them, without art's usual technique of estrangement (Brecht), indirectness and displacement, that is to say, without *mediation*. What is being shown and those who show (do) it are just themselves, are originals as good (or bad) as anyone else. The question to which we do not know the answer as yet is what such directly transmitted directness leads to in the viewers, what this double directness does to the experience of and respect for limits: between others and oneself, between the desirable and the non-desirable, between fantasy and reality (for here everything is given the nature of reality). Crucially, this series of dualisms or distinctions used to be based on that between the private and the public, or the hidden and the displayed. Yet what we witness here is that this distinction is blurred to the point of being extinguished: the private has become public, not per accident, but per programme and thus deliberately and systematically so.

Many reality series (especially the British – tremendously popular – *The Weakest Link*) are based on a vulgar-Darwinist premise: weeding out and removing the weakest, so that the strongest person among the participants is left at the end of the series as the winner. The reality that is depicted and that asks for general approval is that life is everywhere a matter of survival, of 'taking' (out) others before they take you (out). In short, the not-so-subtle message, to which children and young people may be particularly receptive, is that 'it's a jungle out there', making mistrust of others, especially strangers, into an imperative and so displaying mistrust as the basic condition, and expectation, on which to act towards others. This picture of what the real – meaning adult – world is like is also known as 'The Mean World Syndrome', a picture much reinforced by the fact that an average American ten-year-old child has seen some 8,000 simulated murders on TV, making aggression appear as the natural – even inevitable – reaction in the face of frustration (however trifle the resistence that triggers it) and physical violence the natural way of dealing with interpersonal conflict. One's own survival is crowned as having supreme value, as being the only real aim, ignoring all such moral values as care, sympathy and respect; everything else – or more precisely everyone else – is only to be thought of and treated as a means to attain this end.

The same premise appears to apply in the computer games that are now extremely popular. 'When you play computer games, you are the hero in the story, and you are the one who decides if someone is going to die or not. Nearly all the games involve killing as many people as possible. In certain games you get extra points if you make the victim suffer.' This is reported by Stig Rune Lofnes, head of information at the Norwegian organization ChildCare.[35] What does this say about culture in our society? Well, it shows a corner of a complex reality, extremely familiar to some, still unknown to others. I will content myself with pointing out the following. In his book on people's (Americans') conception of evil, C. Fred Alford asked a group of teenagers what they thought about the crimes Adolf Eichmann had committed in connection with the Nazis' extermination of the Jews. What surprised Alford was that a great many of the young people completely avoided answering the question he asked them. What happened? Well, they came up with a series of objections to having to criticize Eichmann's actions, let along condemn them in moral terms. Perhaps one would have done precisely the same as Eichmann? Who knows what Eichmann thought, what his real motivation was? He would certainly have been killed if he had not obeyed the orders of his superiors, wouldn't he? The typical tenor of the responses is that to the extent one is asked to identify with anyone in the scenario of the actor Eichmann and his victims, people identify with Eichmann and do not distance themselves much from him. The effort made consists of seeing oneself in Eichmann's situation, of being in his shoes. In short, the answers exclusively address Eichmann, his victims are altogether left out of the picture, i.e. the very party to the situation which help raise the moral issues that Alford wanted to shed light on, those to do with evil, responsibility and guilt.

It is as if the challenge to reflect on evil, on causing pain and death to others, can be met with satisfactorily by solely making use of *one* standpoint and one perspective, that of the actor, in this case the perpetrator. The young people never visit the victims in their thoughts, let alone their feelings; they do not try to take the place of the victims for so much as a second. Alford's interpretation is this: being a victim – even just fictively and in the imagination – is something that is considered absolutely unbearable, a position one will seek to avoid at any cost. Everything that can be marshalled in the way of intellectual resources is used instead in order to explain – and to a certain degree defend – the course of events, seen from the point of view of the perpetrator. In other words, when pain and suffering come up, it is a question of placing oneself as the one inflicting them, not the one on whom they are inflicted – with the one who is active not passive. It is as if the entire social field is characterized by a 'win or bust' situation, with a corresponding assignment of roles that is just as simple as it is unsubtle and symbolically impoverished; as if the only alternatives consist in having power over others, being able to crush them, or being in the role of someone completely helpless, at the mercy of the superior strength of others. The role of victim becomes synonymous with helplessness, weakness with defeat and death.

I am not saying that the teenagers who identify with Eichmann the perpetrator and do not give his victims one second of their time are sadists. But I am noting that the cast of thought they make use of – win or bust, vanquish or perish – reminds one in its either/or and black/white mentality of the logic of sadism: a logic where the only possible way of dealing with pain in life is to relocate, produce and control it in *others*. What is needed as a corrective is not simply for empathy to be sharpened rather than blunted, so it becomes possible to place oneself spontaneously in the victim's place, rather than (only) the misdoer's. A language is also needed – in the broad sense, not just narrowly verbal and intellectual – to express that the world is not that simple, that the white also has shades of black in it and vice versa, that most things find themselves in the in-between area between extremes, and that violent enactment (neutralizing the other person) is as a rule the least optimum way imaginable of dealing with a conflict – for all parties, it should be noted.

Is there a direct link between computer games and violent films – with the strong-acting survivor as the centre and model of the narrative/plot – and Alford's discovery that teenagers in the United States of the 1990s, as a matter of course and without entertaining any alternatives, respond to moral questions and dilemmas with the aid of explicit identification with the standpoint, motivation and projects of the perpetrator? In the social and cultural field causality is rarely – maybe never – as simple an entity as implied here. But perhaps we have been given something to think about.

Especially in environments characterized by symbolic impoverishment, by the symbolic means to process, put words and images to mental frustration, aggression and conflict being few, coarse and primitive, and where much acquired life-experience would seem to justify viewing the world as a terribly dangerous place to be, where others represent danger and sinister intentions and therefore have to be met with distrust rather than trust and hope, where it is a better survival strategy to be cynical and tough and to attack first than to be trustful and considerate, in short where goodness is weakness and altruism stupidity, the path may prove very short from impulse to action – since impulses from the inside do not have other paths to follow than directly out to what really exists in the outside world. When adult role models – especially male ones – for societal rather than psychological-individual reasons display *physical* means of providing an outlet for pain, for 'resolving' conflicts, as opposed to the symbolic-abstract strategies that a well-functioning culture will provide, it is hardly surprising that violence is handed down from generation to generation as the main – sometimes *only* – experienced path of mastery. Dealing with psychic pain ultimately becomes *synonymous* with the physical enactment and thus the relocation of pain. For lack of symbolic avenues to turn to, both seeking and getting relief become equivalent to physical acting-out.

In environments where violence is the favoured answer to pain, just as violence is the answer to indifference, boredom, uselessness and meaninglessness, an almost imperceptible transition takes place from the first to the last: from pain via indifference to meaninglessness, so that indifference hurts, causes pain, and the lessening or removal of such pain is then sought by shifting it over onto others, who in turn pass it on to yet others in a spiral movement that includes more and more people and where the methods of violence used so as not to be left 'holding the baby' – as the place where the shifting of pain stops, is collected together in all its consequences – become successively more violent and more artful, sophisticated, 'fascinating' – at one and the same time. A situation and an atmosphere are created where violence is both depicted and takes place for no reason. Violence has become so much a matter of course, so everyday and inseparable from existence that no one asks for its *raison d'être* any more: for what it is the answer to. A criminologist records the depiction given by some teenagers of an act of violence in a small town in France:

It is winter in Cergy. Two out-of-work teenagers (about 18) that have an important position among the young people in the neighbourhood, are *en galare*, i.e. hanging around without anything to do. They meet a third teenager, known to be an alcoholic, someone who is in an obvious position of weakness. They jump on him, beat him up, burn him with cigarettes and end up by throwing him, naked and with his hands bound behind his back, into the river Oise. The lad telling me the story finds this very funny. He volunteers no reasons that would justify or explain what happened. What he does emphasize on the other hand are the spectacular aspects of the incident – that the victim was naked, that the water had almost frozen to ice, that he had not had the slightest chance of defending himself. He does not feel that the attackers did anything wrong at all in attacking someone who was normally one of their friends and neighbours. The consequences of their

action were given no attention at all. Everything happens as in a game. The sequences of the incident have
their own logic, but no human characteristics. The
action has its own impetus and intensification. The
boys begin by mishandling the other one slightly, after
which they become progressively involved in increasingly dramatic violence. They end up by trying to take
the life of their victim, without anger but with sophisticated cruelty.[36]

The French sociologist Loic Wacquant places this teenage
violence in a larger political context:

The American ghetto gives us a realistic picture of the
type of social conditions that will probably develop
when the state abandons its essential task of ensuring the
infrastructure that is indispensable for complex urban
communities to be able to function: when the state
fosters a policy that aims at the systematic undermining
of public institutions and allows the development of
market forces and mentality characterized by 'every man
for himself'.[37]

What, then, is violence in the ghetto about? The Norwegian
criminologist Lill Scherdin answers that it can be interpreted
as 'an answer to an abandoned subject', i.e. at finding oneself
in a situation of 'no-future predictability and helplessness'.
She cites her American colleague Elliot Currie's account of
what he refers to as 'the ethos of thoughtlessness', 'a culture
of callousness':

A culture where it is routine to fire people in the name
of 'restructuring' is to an increasing extent being
defined as completely admirable business practice;
where losing one's foothold in the ever more intense

fight for subsistence to an increasing extent opens up the possibility of ending up in a social vacuum, where those who 'lose' are only granted the most elementary support, where even the risk of disability and death depends on income, and basic health offers can be denied those who need them. Where, in short, those at the top always make it clear that they only have minimal concerns for those at the bottom – is a society where the risk of violent crime increases because those who find themselves at the bottom will probably internalize and copy the predominant ethos of callousness. As has been said: 'The person who has been forsaken by everyone can no longer have any feelings towards those who abandon him to his fate.' What we can call a culture of callousness, where concern for the welfare of others is weakened, is not a 'subculture' restricted to young people from the 'lower classes' but a fundamental tendency in the predominant culture itself that the poor young people adopt and beyond a doubt intensify, but which it cannot be said to be the origin of.[38]

As Scherdin comments, the degree of acceptable suffering – where no one intervenes out of an experienced obligation to help – is on the increase for many people in the society being described here. When President Clinton laconically remarked in the early 1990s that 'It is the end of welfare as we know it,' he put his finger on a dawning mentality the consequences of which can hardly be exaggerated: the attitude that various kinds of suffering, need and defeat are to be seen as *self-inflicted* by the individuals concerned. This is the immoral downside of the apparently moral invitation to everyone to be the architect of his own fortune – and according to the same logic, his own *misfortune*. When everything that has to do with responsibility (often called accountability these days, revealingly using a legal word for a moral phenomenon) becomes bound to the individual – individualized – to an extreme degree, the overall impersonal and anonymous causes of increased social misery and the use of violence are lost sight of. The overall framework – the system and its structures – is now no longer criticized; instead, by stripping down to basics, meaning to individuals, everything that is complex and that exerts power over agency and choice, current individual-focused ideology helps protect the political and economic framework against the frustration, rage and protest of those who are the highly personal victims of this impersonal 'modernization', 'rationalization' and 'restructuring'. And so the energy generated by frustration is directed against one's own, or those who are, or have recently become, even lower than oneself on the social ladder. Helplessness as regards the established power hierarchy and impotence as regards the system in its anonymity and impenetrability are compensated for by creating situations of total power and dominance at the micro-level of society, at neighbourhood level, where potential hate-objects, preferably 'strangers' or 'scroungers' or 'losers' (or all at one go, in one and the same person) can at a moment's notice be transformed into *real* hate-objects, with the promise of direct enactment of all accumulated pain. To put it sociologically, the less real power a person or group possesses in the present circumstances, the more that person or group is likely to become an all-too-easy, all-too-present target of the aggression of indiduals deemed as losers in an ever more individualized and competitive society. Those at the top, with power to pull the strings and to occupy the commanding heights within globalized commerce and politics, are effectively beyond the reach of those at the bottom and at the receiving end of their policies.

The violence that occurs in such a situation – a violence that exemplifies the *shifting of pain* in the almost total absence of symbol transformation of it – is one that has its own virtually unstoppable dynamism: one thing leads to the next, 'things just happen', without any clear idea in anyone's mind as to motives or consequences. The search on the part of outsiders – social workers, the police or the judiciary, for example – for a *moral* perspective on all that is taking place is conspicuously absent among, indeed foreign to, those involved, as the story quoted above illustrates. The perspective typically adopted is instead an *aesthetic* one, with the accompanying criteria for assessing if the displayed sequence of aggression is 'spectacular' and 'inventive' or 'amusing'. What is negated in the process is not the conception of a major society of what is good behaviour, so that something intentionally 'wrong' or even 'evil' is done instead. No, what is denied is ennui, boredom, lack of meaning, the fact that nothing means anything and that nothing meaningful takes place. Participation in particularly 'inventive' or reckless violence promises a break with this experience, even if only a brief respite. The expressions used to add something distinctive to the *performance* of the person perpetrating violence use aesthetic rather than moralizing (and thus possibly censuring) vocabulary. To get the adrenaline pumping becomes an end in itself, as does the excitement.

The fact that tormenting others is punishable seems unimportant. What matters is the prospect of having fun, of fifteen minutes of fame. For one thing that is certain is that there will be no lack of attention paid to young people who are behind particularly inventive acts of violence that result in death. The German journalist Regina General lists three highlights in the course of two randomly chosen weeks' media coverage of serious youth crime in present-day Germany.[39] In the first instance, the offender is a twenty-year-old man, inconspicuous, apparently friendly and likeable. Stated desired occupation: killer. Executed deed: the murder of two old ladies. In the second instance, five friends are before the court, accused of having throttled a neighbour until he died. Stated motive: some more money to buy liquor. They state that the amount they receive in reduced social aid is insufficient. Something has to be done to get hold of what is needed. In the third instance, half of the students of a vocational school class are accused of sexual abuse of a fellow-student and to have placed the worst of their perversities on the Internet, with thousands of hits and considerable demand from the general public as a result.

The journalist reports that youth crime shows no signs of being on the increase at the moment in Germany. That is not the point. The changes she thinks she can observe lie somewhere else and are highly relevant for our theme. It is the way violent crime is perceived and marketed that is changing. The perpetrators can guarantee getting considerable publicity – a state they would normally not achieve via their 'usual' activities. It has to do with being the centre of attention for all those in society who otherwise would not be the slightest bit interested in such young people and the lives they lead. There have been several cases, particularly in Germany, with the famous tragedies in the United States such as the massacre at Columbine High School as a possible model, where so-called *Amokläufer* – always young lads – break out of their 'young lad' space heavily armed with automatic weapons, the deadly use of which they have learned from dozens of violent videos, and launch into a killing spree by storming into a school to 'take out' students and teachers. Though often taken by the public to happen impulsively – say, due to some recently suffered setback or insult – subsequent police investigation typically concludes that the killing spree and the identities and number of its victims have in fact been premeditated in great detail by the young killer, often for months or even years.

We like to talk in our society about optimum opportunities for development, not least for the young. Such opportunities are often a rare commodity (or the converse, where young people are bombarded with so many of them that they are confused and become indifferent, lose their direction and are incapable of making decisions – on which more later). For many young people, the future is simply a black hole. Something higher or more long-term than the next 'rush', the experience of being 'high' again along with some friends, does not exist. What is behind this? Perhaps it is a real misunderstanding on the part of society, a collective category error that is displaying one of its consequences here – that it must be permissible to seek one's own satisfaction at any price. As society now is, as it appears to those who are young and who notice what the adult world *does*, it appears to have an overall message, one to be found across the board as a uniting theme: never share with anyone. *We* never pays off – all that pays off is *I*. It does not pay off to take care of others, only to take care of oneself. The one who deceives is only exploiting his chance; the one who does not, has no chance, or is too naïve or ignorant to have understood the basic rules of the game.

Much is going wrong between the generations. A word such as 'upbringing' has in many circles – among adults as well as young people – something cramped about it, something old-fashioned and moralistic, something superior and anti-progressive. To try to pass on moral values to one's own children is becoming increasingly difficult, among other things because parental authority is being challenged from many directions – not least by advertising aimed at children and tailor-made to forge an alliance against adults said to 'know nothing' about what children desire these days – and because 'negotiations' and compromises are a dominant trend in much popular pedagogical thinking. Moreover, to be an adult that tries to communicate standards of right and wrong to other people's children (as well as one's own) is regarded in many circles as almost wrong in principle; examples from everyday life indicate that overt correction of other children's behaviour will soon be considered taboo, with the adult bearing the entire burden of proof in the event of conflict, and with the corrected child as the offended party, with every prospect of getting support from its own 'liberal' parents. Indeed, it is becoming rare for adults to initiate conversation – meaning a friendly one – with children not their own. Today's ten- or thirteen-year-olds report that it virtually never happens that a so-called 'stranger', be it on the street or the bus seat next to one, makes contact at all. Children are for the most part taught that strangers will often be dangerous, anything but well meaning and deserving of trust. Everything to do with how to behave, with intervention in cases even of one child's visibly molesting and abusing another, is – so the prevalent attitude has it – to be left either exclusively to the child's parents or to some professional personnel assigned to the task. As a consequence, the social world as one in which children and teenagers experience active and reciprocal communication, including a lively exchange of experiences, attitudes and values, is radically shrinking – at the peril of all involved, meaning all three generations. It is as if all people who are now deemed 'outsiders' to the child in question have no purchase on the codes of conduct that its actions are expected to conform to. Relativism abounds, plurality of life-views and lifestyles is the name of the game, and it takes enormous confidence on the part of an 'outsider' to engage actively in cases of conflict – not to mention bullying – between children. From an early age young people learn to follow the requirement – and thereby everyone's right to – 'self-realization', which they see that adults are so obsessed with – if not in word, then in deed. And what about those who are old – really old? Well, they cost money, they are expensive and work-intensive to keep going, an item of expenditure that is always on the increase. What is more, they do not understand the rules that now apply. They think in terms of their own youth long ago, their experiences and values coloured by a society that no longer exists – a society where duty went before rights, where what one *had* to do was far more important than what the individual *chose* to do – if there ever was a choice.

Many young violent criminals are characterized by their lack of remorse – not only do they not show remorse but they cannot comprehend *why* anyone should be interested in it. Isn't making a career as a professional killer a quick way of earning lots of money and fame and thus of achieving aims that are recognized by society? Even in cases of spectacular bestiality those who have taken part claim that no one really wanted to hurt anyone else. The motives professed are anything but sadistic or deeply personal; they do not involve strong feelings or carefully considered aims. The tormenting of others is excitement, a little extra fun – after all, there are so few 'extras' one allows oneself. The opportunity was there – what else do you need to know? And if pressed, the fallback position is always available, in the form of the conversation-ending counter-question: who are you to dare to criticize? Who has the right to correct the behaviour of others? Indeed, who is entitled to judge and to criticize?[40]

Have I now proved my assertion that culture is failing in its task, as defined above?

In its original form, the assertion can be seen as an untenable simplification. It gets hold of certain characteristics of present-day reality but misses others. Which? Two qualifications are necessary: first, the culture of a society such as ours is not at all an unambiguous, homogeneous entity but a many-headed affair. Culture comprises many phenomena, expressions and tendencies; these appear alongside each other, even though they are often incompatible. But the point is that they *can* perfectly well exist parallel to each other, without necessarily creating conflict or excluding each other. Why? Partly because – and this is qualification number two – culture has just as many (and diverse) addressees, users and practitioners as it itself is diverse and non-uniform. Sociologically speaking, this is referred to as different social classes within the same major society practising and mediating 'its' respective cultures, understood as ways of doing things and of interpreting things with the aid of symbolic-linguistic effects and media (to allude to the French sociologist Pierre Bourdieu and his famous notion of habitus).[41]

Where do these qualifications take us in regard to the question of culture failing its task? My answer is that one cannot hold that *culture as such* fails in its task to give all members of society good symbolic-linguistic resources for dealing with the whole range of challenges, trials and crises that human life contains – in short: to meet pain in life (that of others and one's own) without creating more of it, intensifying it, passing it on. The reason for this is not just the obvious one that culture – in the singular – does not exist; that there are as dissimilar transmitters as there are receivers, to use that language. What is relevant for our discussion is that what there is in the way of good symbolic resources – everything from literature via fairytales to drama, film, dancing, music, painting, etc. – does not reach its destination so as to be used by the people and groups of people who perhaps need these resources – for handling and alleviating pain – most of all. Note that this statement is not exclusively intended for the underprivileged in our society – whether it be those with little education, no work, the poor, drug addicts, etc. As we will see in the next chapter, among the declared 'resource-strong' – those in the middle of life, with a strongly ascending career curve and likewise salary – there are also clear signs of a lack of being in touch with the most difficult sides of life, with defeat, loss and adversity. It is as if those who have specialized in an existence on the sunny side of life, on the ascent of the high summits, those only reached by a few and only after a particularly hard effort, turn out to be just as poor and helpless at the instant the crisis should happen to strike and they are suddenly caught up with by the realities of the drawbacks of life. It is a question of a lack of practice – biographically as well as symbolically, physically as well as mentally – in looking such fundamental conditions as dependency, vulnerability and mortality in the eye, i.e. the characteristics of existence one has not been in contact with for so long (right up until the acute crisis, perhaps) and has not needed to have an attitude towards. Why should a drug addict not have just as great a competence in this area as a business director, the man who is now in an existential free-fall after his marriage has broken up or his company gone down the tube? At the moment of crisis low culture can be existentially just as resilient, just as symbolically saturated with meaning, just as wise as high culture: a Janis Joplin just as true to reality as an Edvard Munch or a Marcel Proust.

What, then, is the danger? There are many dangers, not only those usually most discussed such as the unequal access for different classes and environments to the finest treasures of culture(s) and the most durable expressions, as the differences in this approach increase systematically according to the general increase in economic-material differences between those who have most and those who have least. As mentioned, I see no direct correlation between wealth defined socio-economically and wealth as a share of, knowledge of and use of vital symbolic resources: in that respect the rich may prove to be poor and the poor rich. The danger I wish to indicate here is, however, of a different nature than one that is suited to statistical overviews. It consists in a *fear of seriousness*. The Swedish film creator Roy Andersson puts it like this:

> With the word seriousness I am thinking of taking things seriously, doing things properly, getting to the bottom of things, taking consequences, making things clear – something that does not in the slightest involve grumpy looks or an absence of fun. In

many ways I believe that our lives – indeed, our whole society – are characterized by a fear of seriousness and a hatred of quality . . . Expressions of quality and seriousness remind us of this fact, and since they occur so rarely, they are surprising and discomforting reminders of the prevalent skimping and superficiality. This creates aggression.[42]

TWELVE

Pain as Compulsive Choice in a Multi-option Society

In present-day Western societies there is a widespread belief that the individual – and nowadays everything begins and ends with the individual – desires freedom more than anything else, in the sense of individual self-realization. Freedom understood in that way, lived in that way, has many problematic aspects that have much to do with the creation and shifting of pain. The developments we have witnessed over the past couple of decades lead to various forms of social pathologies. What is it that creates such pathologies?

My assertion – which is, of course, only part of the answer – is that an increasing number of the pathologies I am talking about are created by choice becoming compulsory in a multi-option society. Pathologies such as burn-out, action paralysis, anxiety and depression can be considered as unintentional consequences of social conditions that are otherwise perceived to be conducive to the individualistic realization of freedom. Key words for the conditions I am referring to are mobility, flexibility and adaptability. *Readjustment* is at the heart of this, taken as a demand targeted at each individual that he or she needs to internalize and prove loyal to at all times and across the entire social board, as it were. While the prevalent ideology of our time, neo-liberalism, would have the conditions mentioned above represent positive conditions for realizing freedom, my assertion is that the converse applies: because these conditions are imposed on individuals and force them constantly to choose, and constantly to choose right, and constantly to update and thereby annul previous choices, individuals reach an impasse of non-freedom rather than any real freedom – an impasse of exhaustion and self-coercion rather than an expression of creativity and individuality. Furthermore, individual identity is not/no longer seen as an expression of an essence, something that is fixed and constant. Instead, identity – we are told by all sorts of pundits who have their finger on the pulse of things – has to do with something that is completely *constructed* – something fluid, plastic and staged, something heterogeneous and multi-dimensional (identity is 'pluralized' when the roles and arenas are multiplied, etc.). Nevertheless, this newly won 'freedom' to constantly recreate oneself comes at a high price – as we shall see.

The consequence of this trend is not that people are becoming increasingly egoistic and less altruistic. This dichotomy misses the point; it misses what is novel here. The simple contrast between egoism and altruism is breaking down, in the sense that the compulsory choices of the multi-option society force the individual to ruthlessly exploit *himself* – something that is bad not only for the individual himself but also for his capacity to show concern for others, to have any kind of *surplus* of involvement, initiative and strength left for other people – especially those who are striving themselves. Social pressure on the individual – adapt, adapt – is internalized and finds expression in the individual's merciless and restless pressure on himself, so that healthy self-assertion – mental and emotional 'taking care of oneself', paying attention to one's own vulnerability and the limits for one's stamina – suffers as a result, as does one's ability to care for others. The ability to care that we are dealing with here is both for oneself and for others. In the former instance it has to do with how the individual behaves towards himself in a broad psychological sense: what he demands of himself in the form of making choices that indicate mastery and success, which needs he gives priority to, and which he rejects, plays down or represses.

To be happy or successful (can we appreciate the difference?) has become a requirement, something everyone believes is a god-given right. And it is without a doubt a historical fact that people in today's Western and materially speaking rich societies generally perceive that the possibilities for realizing themselves are constantly improving. The *options* multiply, the opportunities are literally unlimited – there is a plethora of them and the only thing to make sure of is that *I* choose the right thing. 'Only thing'? With the increase in potential choices, the compulsion to choose also increases. The fall is greater, and the safety net increasingly coarse-meshed and fragile. The individual has to take the consequences of his own choice. Doesn't that sound reasonable? Is there anything wrong in that? Isn't precisely that a sign of progress when it comes to freedom and responsibility?

In one sense, yes; in other respects, no. For a start, and even though it has become politically incorrect to observe so, the fact is that for an individual agent to realize his *de jure* freedom, resources in a comprehensive sense – involving economic capital no less than the fashionable cultural one – are required and such material resources still tend to be distributed along lines of class, notwithstanding assertions to the contrary, and according to which radically individualized human resources constitute the only difference that now truly makes a difference – that between winning or losing.[43] In a society where the reign of the collective and the great narratives is past, where the individual has been 'liberated' from the yoke of tradition and religion, where there is no longer any 'as father, so son' compulsion, where the older generation abdicate their authority regarding the younger generation – in such a society the downsides of gaining freedom, in an individualistic sense, are often lost from view, although not *clinically* lost, not psychosomatically. It is *here* that the downsides are intercepted, here they are stored – well understood *or* misinterpreted as they may be by the individual himself and by the current interpretations and values of society at large.

I acknowledge that a great many people tackle the challenges of a societal era of adaptation and freedom/coercion of choice quite well. There is no lack of examples demonstrating that laying aside old competences and acquiring new ones often results in personal enrichment and is a source of growth and wellbeing; in short, a chance that previous ages did not offer people to make use of new facets of themselves. For that reason there is often a good match between what dynamism in working life calls for and what the individual experiences as stimulating. In addition, it is important to point out that many people manage to get through things well if a crisis or a defeat should occur – not only by virtue of their own resources but also thanks to unselfish efforts by friends, colleagues and life-partners. In short, there is a vital in-between area between the individual and the companies or institutions, an area consisting of a network and environments that can help contain individuals about to crash. It is perhaps in the nature of things that this interception and backing-up rarely reaches the front pages of the newspapers or becomes a theme for popular academic study; there is something silent about the phenomenon we are dealing with here, about, say, the continued importance of friendship, unlike the visibility attached to such defined problems as a marked increase in eating disorders among young people or in the use of Prozac among get-ahead 30-year-olds. Everything that is doing well, or is prevented from going wrong, does not really come to light, compared to what really goes awry.

In other words, there is much positive mastery – at both individual and group level – in so-called option society. But my aim in this book is not to dwell on this but instead on where *pain* is created, shifted and enacted. I turn my attention in that direction – and find a great deal.

I am thinking about the signs of an increase in factors that contribute to the individual experiencing the more rigorous expectations regarding self-realization in the outside world as an ever greater *burden*, as something that involves major mental strain. When being happy has become a requirement, when being successful is so too, something happens to the gained freedom that previous generations and societies did not have: increased freedom becomes increased strain. It has to do with many simultaneous trends, most of which I cannot do justice to in this discussion: among other things, how we in the space of two decades have gone from welfare as we knew it to minimum effort based on the ideology of self-inflictedness and self-sufficiency, so that the person ending up in unemployment or the dole queue is under pressure to get out of this situation as soon as possible. Fundamental conditions that simply have to do with being a human being, especially dependency and vulnerability, have acquired an imbalance that is unambiguously negative: to be *in need*, to need the help and care of other people, is seen as morally suspect in itself, a state that ought to be as short-lived as possible and that society at large in general and 'the public sector' in particular must not fuel under any circumstances – perhaps avoiding it through propping up those in need with state benefits. Dependency and vulnerability nowadays tend to be associated with *shame*, with revealing something about oneself that ought not to be displayed and ought not to be there in the first place.

The Norwegian psychiatrist Finn Skårderud puts his finger on the relationship between cultural change and a change in the feeling of shame. Traditional shame in the form of embarrassment is on the decline. Nevertheless 'the story of present-day Western culture [is] not that of a lost shame but rather of a *transported* shame.' This formulation accords well with the picture I have tried to present. As Skårderud makes clear, the most important transportation – and change – is from a collective to an individual norm. The transportation of shame towards the individual and his psychological register and resources does not mean that shame disappears, but that 'we lose a language about it. Shame becomes more silent and more lonely. It becomes less distinct.'[44] Why less distinct? One of the main reasons is that the premises and ideals of our age's one-sided preoccupation with self-development are unclear. For what is self-realization when it comes to it? What is authenticity? Are there undisputable and generally valid standards to go by? How can the individual feel certain of having reached the goal?

There are no simple answers here, no answers that remove the individual's doubt about the tenability of his own efforts and performance, let alone the never really overcome doubt: am I good enough? The situation is indeed confusing and ambiguous. On the one hand, much would seem to indicate that the form of individualization we are talking about has increased with subjectivism and relativism as a result. A striking sign that this is true is how difficult it has become in our society to *criticize* the choices of action another person makes. What right have I to criticize your choices, your preferences, your values and ideals? Especially explicitly moral criticism, with a tinge of condemnation (other people's private consumption, for example) constantly runs the risk of being perceived as *moralistic*, as a paternalistic 'know-all' attitude, i.e. something everyone would like to be spared. To have the nerve just to come here and interfere, without being asked, in *my* private decisions and preferences – who is entitled to such mingling with the affairs of others? What is reprehensible is not the object of the criticism. It has been shifted from the object or issue to the criticizer, or more precisely to a person at all raising any criticism of others' actions. Individualization in general and the ideal of authenticity in particular are undermining the potential of criticism and correctives, because issue and person are now so intimately interwoven – in terms of both experience and norm – that the former division between them disappears. Correction has almost become synonymous with molestation.

However, this – conventionally culture-critical – picture is far from being the whole story. With the aid of Skårderud, we can see that although the moral practice of criticizing the behaviour of others has become more difficult, this does not necessarily mean the end of shame in our culture. The basic structure of shame remains intact: shame about oneself in relation to the other/others. All the same, what is changing is the three instances that constitute and determine the structure of shame in a *lived*, psychological sense, namely, the self, others, and the culture that mediates the relationship between the former two. Modern culture is open. Therefore, more possibilities means an endless number of alternatives but at the same time, fewer sheet anchors, less clarity, less unambiguity and objectivity – and limits that become increasingly *unclear*. Just as in previous ages, shame, as Skårderud says, is 'an affect that, consciously or unconsciously, is fuelled by the discrepancy between self-ideal and realization. Shame emerges from this tension between how I wish to be perceived and how I feel that I am perceived.'[45] The radical openness of culture, its porous nature, its quality of being a melting-pot for the new, for all sorts of change, means that the individual is thrown back on himself and his own ongoing *choices* of cultural yardsticks – knowing full well that all such supra-individual references are themselves in a process of restless change and are therefore unable to provide the individual with a *hold*, something firm to hold on to in his efforts to ascertain whether he is being successful in his self-realization.

Neither party has the answer. To be thrown back on oneself and one's own resources, since culture – like the omnipresent market – is constantly supplying new option portfolios rather than answers and yardsticks, means being reminded of one's own dependency and vulnerability, one's own aloneness in the throes of choices, because it now becomes apparent that mastery cannot be attained by relying solely on one's own, individualistically conceived resources from one's own breast. Independence and autonomy begin to crack, to betray the fact that they are not what is given, but presuppose more profound and underlying fundamental conditions, conditions that reveal that the self-realization project in an individualistic sense is an illusion, and a dangerous one at that. The uncovering of this arrogance causes pain, pain in the form of shame that is fuelled by a sense of sub-optimal performance, by not realizing enough of one's presumed potential: my shame is more about *myself* than towards the other/others. Shame takes the form of self-conflict – manifested as self-disgust, as strict self-control regimes such as eating disorders, or sadomasochistic sex, or piercing or other forms of self-injury – more than the conflicts of the individual with others or the major society, a conflict traditionally fuelled by the individual realizing 'too much', by way of transgressing limits of behaviour and violating standards of conduct established by tradition and upheld by the 'collective conscious' of society (to refer to the perspective of Emile Durkheim's classic work *The Suicide*).[46]

In times of violent societal changes that individuals do not perceive they can influence themselves, changes of the type they feel they are subject to and steamrollered by, it becomes a question of finding *something* at any rate that can be brought under complete control, *something* that allows the feeling of powerlessness to be replaced by a feeling of power and actual control, where *I* do the forming rather than *being formed* – even if the price of gaining such control means, among other things, withdrawing from the big, unsafe world out there to what is close and my own – to I, me, mine: depoliticization and narcissism as two sides of the same process.

What could be more natural in such a situation than to focus on the *body*? After all, the body is mine, it is myself. The 'artists of starving' that Skårderud writes about illustrate an outcome of what I am referring to. The anorexic girl who walks *past* the outdoor restaurant where all the others are sitting stuffing themselves with rich food, with their bodies distending, can experience this moment, this eminently visible contrast, as proof of her own sovereignty and power and of other people's weakness. To form the body, to compel it, to conquer one's needs and their dictates, to let the will decide over or regularly set everything 'natural' and biological out of action, is one of the many possible interpretations of people who present it as a choice – against the large backdrop of all that is non-chosen, that which is inflicted or imposed on one's life – to place everything to do with the body under a particularly strict regime of self-control where the body is punished or rewarded, depending on the nature of the disorder, in its enforced subservience to its lord and master. Interpreted as an extreme exercise in self-control, the need to control manifested here is something that calls for an explanation, that reveals that something has got completely *out of* control, so that the attempt to control the body compensates for a loss of control – a mastery strategy precipitated by powerlessness.

Applied to the youth violence we mentioned earlier: inconsideration towards others can go hand in hand with inconsideration towards oneself. The lack of care for others can exist side by side with a lack of care for oneself. Hardness towards others – often expressed as cynicism – is fuelled by working hard to be hard towards oneself. More profoundly, it is fuelled by denying, by trying to eradicate one's own vulnerability. For vulnerability, one's own no less than that of others, is now looked upon as identical with weakness. And weakness is what this world will not tolerate, because this world is all about each and everyone's survival, that is to say, being strong and fighting so as always to come out on top. Moral admonishment regarding this way of 'reading' our society and claiming that egoism now rules supreme is to miss the point. Of course, I believe that the type of violence we are dealing with here in the examples from Germany must be condemned and punished. Of course, the guilty have a responsibility they must assume and that no analysis of society can alter. Let that be quite clear.

What we have to examine in greater depth, once the condemnation has been voiced and the courts have had their say, is the question of 'Why?' Leading on from the perspective adopted in this book, a possible explanation is offered by understanding such violence as the shifting of psychic pain. We know that the young people involved here in many cases indulge in self-injury as well as inflicting violence on concrete individuals. In both cases, limits are being transcended, put out of action; it is possibly the case that only the limits that one has created oneself are respected, those which by an act of will one has chosen. Seen in this way, the young people perhaps illustrate a more overlapping, widespread phenomenon than the one that has directly to do with violent crime and its causes: the fact that we live in a society that generally speaking has a sinking understanding and acceptance of limits of the kind that people – those who clash with and are subject to limits – have not created by a personal act of will, in the sense of having been able to *choose*. We only want to know about what we can choose for ourselves – and de-choose everything else.

The individuals that the capitalist economy requests in an age of neoliberalism, where the trend is for the whole of society with all its various organized activities to be transformed into a marketplace and arenas for everything that is consigned the nature of a commodity, have, to use a psychological term, weak egos. The individuals requested today are not strong-willed, independent-minded and autonomous, true to their own ideas; rather, they are heteronomous, driven by anxiety and insecurity and so easily manipulated by outside forces. The paradox is not to be denied: though this is often declared the era of individualism, conformism – in the gestalt of the individual's obsession with adapting to the demands addressing him, especially in the workplace – is tightening its grip.

As convincingly shown in rich detail in C. Fred Alford's book *Whistleblowers: Broken Lives and Organizational Power*, individuals who take the ethos of individualism at its word and who take an independent stand on ethically sensitive issues, for instance by openly protesting against unethical policies practised by their own organization, are typically met with a whole battery of devices of rejection, being frozen out by colleagues and being ignored by those at the top, thus setting in motion a process often ending with the autonomous individual being declared psychologically unstable and unfit to continue work for the corporation in question.[47] As Alford documents from the United States, where he did interviews with whistleblowers, a ruined life – a lost job, a lost home, a lost family – is quite often the (rarely anticipated) price of defying the powers that be in the name of autonomous judgment. Such individuals are not heroes but a pain in the arse, exploited by bosses as a warning and despised by colleagues who have their own lack of nerve put into sharp relief by the protester in their midst. So much for the ideology hailing the independent-minded individual! The alarming thing is that the individuals, to the extent to which they make an effort to adapt to the demands for change (in education, in the labour market, in their private lives and love-lives), are in danger of considering and treating other human beings as means rather than as ends in themselves.

Furthermore, I am claiming that the 'flexible', adaptable and change-willing individual we are dealing with is in danger of turning *himself* exclusively into a means – not just others – that is to say, a means for intentions and interests that are not the individual's own but that have been taken over and internalized from market players and advertisements that intensify seeing human beings as commodities, so that all that is human – all needs, all aims, all fantasies – can become the object of satisfaction, meaning instant and always available (accessible) gratification, by being transformed into so many commodities. Ultimately, this imposed commodity nature – how much something is worth and for what price it can be sold, measured on the basis of a demonstrated demand – will become characteristic of all of existence. From a critical point of view, it must be said that the optimally change-willing and adaptable individual – the one who in all his doings 'is' just as flexible as the changing outside world it has to adapt to so as not to fall off, fall outside – is the unfree, non-autonomous, weak-egoed individual perceived as not only willing to treat others as means, and thus inconsiderately, but also to make himself – as a mind and a body – the object of just as gross inconsideration.

The attitude to the self in such a situation is one of ruthless exploitation. And this exploitation creates pain, the pain creates a need of mastery now typically understood as removal, and the removal of pain creates a need for containers, for someone out there who is suitable for housing it. In short, the pain *in* the subject creates and exerts pressure on the subject's relations to other people and the outside world in general. Alternatively, if others are not available for this purpose, or we are dealing with a person with a genuine concern for others, the pain in a self will be locked inside the self-relation, with various types of self-destructive behaviour as a probable consequence.

A provocative question: is there a link between the teenager with a drug problem who engages in self-injury, who slices his own skin with a knife, who forces himself to cut slightly more, slightly larger, slightly deeper than the last time, and the businessman who walks slightly faster, almost breaks into a run, checks his watch for the umpteenth time: will I reach the plane, the meeting in time, will I land the contract for the company, what will my boss say if it falls through, how much have I actually slept this week, when was I last out with the kids? Two modern persons, side by side in the same society, but miles apart on the basis of outer characteristics to do with status and success? Or not so far apart after all? Father and son, perhaps?

The two of them are at opposite ends of the spectrum, admittedly. They belong to vastly different environments, have different goals, command few and many resources respectively. The drop-out kid and the go-ahead businessman in his prime and for whom everything is possible. But are they so different? Are there no resemblances? Yes, perhaps the fact that both are exploiting themselves, pushing themselves, making themselves hard, and both, apparently, can put up with more and more – mind and body, two in one – and who get increasingly hard and, apparently, can withstand more and more. The stimuli have to be intensified to get 'high' again, yesterday's excesses and new conquests have to be constantly replaced by new ones, stronger ones, if there is to be any chance of a new kick – perhaps not totally unrelated to how earlier career success has to be topped by advances characterized by even greater boldness, risk-taking, falls – much at stake, yes, but it has to be so if one is to feel alive. How much can I put up with? To what extent can I surpass myself, exceed previous merits and records?

Produce the pain in your life. Endure it. Don't expose yourself to other people's – in a double sense: the pain others have, and that is theirs, not mine; and the pain they might inflict on me, if I do not protect myself. The same strategy is used in both cases: to harden myself – against myself and self-inflicted pain no less than any inflicted from outside. Pain is a sign of being alive. But living and being able to go on with life does not have to do with pain as such. It has to do with withstanding it, more precisely with constantly being willing to do what can be done to be better able to withstand it: the pain limit. Yes, what about it? It is my ability to withstand, that's what it is. To live is to be able to experience pain: so I must be able to withstand pain so as to put up with life. So it is not at all a matter of denying or repressing the presence of pain in existence. No, it is a question of mastery, as it is of most things at present: of training myself to take my sensitivity to pain in my own hands, making it a project to shift the point where pain feels completely intolerable, to stretch it farther and farther forward: formerly, the point it became intolerable was *there*, now it is *here*. And I figure I still have considerable potential for improvement.

In other words: I am vulnerable, much as I don't like to admit it. But what I do is to subdue my vulnerability, in the form of a pain level. I compel it, seek to gain control over it by dictating its meaning and power over me, in my life.

Is this a true picture? Don't solemn CEOs tell us that we are a nation of wimps, of people always complaining of being ill and worn-out for no reason, who can put up with less and less – with all the negative spin-off effects this has on our productivity, with the burdens it imposes on our social budgets and our health service? Isn't it high time someone did something about the economic catastrophes absence from work is causing?

Can we withstand less pain than before, or less than what we – based on an assessment that at some point has to be normative – ought to be able to withstand? Or do we withstand more than before, in the sense described of having become our own worst slave-drivers, of carrying out psychosomatic exploitation on ourselves, so that our capacity is stretched *a little* more, like the famous elastic band – the one that we both are and that we stretch? Or is it perhaps not so simple as the one description killing off the other?

I do not think the descriptions completely exclude each other. The fluctuations in absence from work and its causes are not something I am qualified to determine. The director and like-minded people in business life and politics are putting out an unambiguous message, even though the diagnosis on which they base themselves may prove to be erroneous: the message that each and every one of us must demand more of himself, must push himself to ever greater efforts than is now (presumably) the case. And it is a signal that the businessman we outlined has taken in – an internalization that can have far more illness-provoking consequences than the person concerned is prepared for.

As mentioned earlier: a lot of successful coping is taking place in the encounter with the challenges I am depicting. My analysis is deliberately selective by dwelling on the pain that is created in cases where the ability to master it and the resources available fall short, partly because of the influence of the powerful ideological view of our age that the individual ought to tackle his own problems and that to say to others 'Look, here is my pain, here is my vulnerability' involves a shame-inducing defeat and betrays a weakness that each and every one of us would prefer to hide and deny rather than openly admit.

One thing has been well documented in recent years: the number of emergency cases in psychiatry has led to an increase in the number of people hospitalized and treated who belong to the category 'go-ahead men in their prime', men with high status on the basis of all socio-economic criteria who after a period of overloading in their job and in their career/family life suffer a terrible crash and flatten out completely. What is the overall picture such a phenomenon has to be placed in if we are to understand its societal significance, what warning signal is it sending?

The development of society I am referring to has to do with how readiness to change replaces perseverance and integrity as a core virtue, especially among employees in the private sector – though in our times of privatization increasingly also in the public sector. To the extent to which a present-day employee is encouraged to show loyalty (an honourable virtue), this loyalty is towards economic targets to do with increased production and increased profit; or alternatively towards projects that are often short-term and a working environment that at any moment can have its staff downsized or outsourced: this represents a reality that is taking over an increasing number of sectors and employees, and that is undermining loyalty understood as long-term obligation to companies that are stable, secure and place-bound.[48] To 'improve competitiveness' stops being a means to a higher end and becomes an end in itself: a system imperative coming from the outside that everyone has to submit to. Structural changes and their enormous dynamics in today's turbo-capitalism are the silent but incredibly power-concentrated origin of presented, 'given' requirements that each and every individual has to adapt to as best they can, each alone. A major consequence of individualization in our age is that the cause, no less than the symptoms (being burnt-out, lonely, impotent, apathetic, feeling a loss of meaning, being depressed), appears in an individualized rather than a political-structural form, i.e. as depending on the individual, as self-inflicted, and as a sign of failure or neglect, or lack of effort. The German sociologist Ulrich Beck has put it like this: in our society economic-systematic contradictions and conflicts are transformed into biographical and individual 'mistakes', into shortcomings of the kind for which the individual only has himself to thank – blame.[49]

This gives the following picture. While former generations became ill because of a disciplining that prevented them from forming and pursuing their own aims and ideals, the people of today's *option generation* become ill because of having to choose between too many possibilities. The downside of the much-celebrated freedom of choice is that choice becomes compulsory: choice is the one activity from which the individual enjoys no escape, no break, no exit. The overproduction of possibilities by the option society – here you have all possible types of education and training to choose between, all sorts of occupations, lifestyles, identities – so that everything is possible, given the multiplying of alternatives provided by the market in terms of commodities – is not a luxury problem, tempting as it may be to see it as such. The normatively charged requirement to realize one's capacities and assume responsibility for one's own life – life understood as the accumulatively produced sum of all the choices made – has within a relatively short time become so intense and omnipresent that it now produces considerable amounts of pain: it contributes to making individuals ill who have internalized the requirement. With the Danish sociologist Rasmus Willig we can talk about 'an internal tribunal where individuals have to defend their lack of skills and proficiencies regarding the normative expectations of the option society'. The question is: isn't this defence work exhausting in itself? Willig comments:

> The omnipresent suffering from indeterminacy (Hegel's *Leiden an Unbestimmtheit*), the suffering involved in putting up with changes as the only thing that is permanent, in always having to be in motion, thereby emerges and places the individual in a position of insufficiency where he is left with an eroded self. The fact that the individual has to maintain the illusion of everything being possible leads to personal exhaustion.[50]

We can now glimpse the price that has to be paid for contemporary society's advocated, even dictated, form of self-realization. It has to do with the price that arises by the focus – all demands, all psychological and mental energy – being directed at *the self* and not, as in previous ages, at collectively handed-down contexts of order that the individual could gain support from to a great (although varying) extent, in an elementary assurance of his identity, his social roles and his worth – these experienced as relatively stable entities, as something that was fixed, and out of reach of dramatic shifts and changes. Now, on the other hand, the individual's orientation has made an about turn, zooming in on the resources of the self, the so-called 'human capital' said to reside in each individual (employee), the cultivation of which – for competitive success in the marketplace – is hailed as the prerogative of its individual bearer. The freedom always to be able to choose turns into a compulsion to choose the right thing, into a fear of taking a wrong turning at the ever-growing series of crossroads that make up contemporary social existence, and so risking losing momentum vis-à-vis one's competitors.

The change in mentality I am referring to has made a considerable impact on psychotherapeutic practices. From my point of view the changes here attest to comprehensive cultural change. The 'guilty' and conscience-stricken individual that Freud placed at the centre of his analyses, where the neurosis bears witness to the mental pressure from the conflict between the individual's desire and what the norms of society allow and forbid respectively (internalized in the voice of the superego), is in the process of disappearing – from theories as well as from therapy. Present-day individuals do not concentrate on the division between obedience and prohibition, but on that between *the possible and the impossible* – the point being that the division is perfectly fluid and open to never-ceasing alteration, making it imperative that the individual learns to negotiate it deftly. What turns out to be possible, and what impossible, is precisely a question of one's own ability to seize the initiative in a world where 'everything' is said to be possible, as long as the individual can make full use of his inner resources. Society or the 'system' cannot be blamed for wrong choices or untried possibilities; the individual only has himself to thank, whether he succeeds or fails.

To be sure, present-day men and women have liberated themselves from morals in the conventional sense that applied at the time of Freud. The fear of outer coercion, in the form of clear prohibitions indicated by unambiguous authorities, has been replaced by the fear of self-inflicted failure, of one's own limitations. The opening up of possibilities and emphasis on the all-overshadowing importance of individual initiative for all of life's areas means that human beings have set themselves in motion. The very meaning of being a human being, of what identity qua being human centres on, is up for grabs. Nothing is laid down once and for all. Nature is no longer an unchanging reference and instance – neither nature in the subject nor that outside, as novel technologies allow us to intervene into both realms – or objects – in an object-altering manner unthinkable until recently. Nor is there any longer any fixed and normative reference of a transcendental nature, in the form of a god that sets moral limits and maintains an order. In this context the French psychiatrist and sociologist Alain Ehrenberg notes that 'depression is melancholy in a society where everyone is equal and free; depression is the illness par excellence in democracies and market economies'.[51] Depression is the downside of the sovereignty man has achieved via civilization, i.e. with the one who is paralysed by possibilities and unable to act, rather than the one who acts in the (morally) wrong way. As the moral forms of compulsion decline (understood as compulsion in the tension and conflict between individual and society – think of Freud once more), the purely *intrapsychic* forms of compulsion increase: the coercion the subject imposes on himself. The yardstick of depression is not made up of individual-transcending ideas about justice but of the displayed ability to act; not of suffering under pressure from outside authorities in a world where so much is forbidden and out of reach but by the individual's revealed fallibility in making optimal choices in a world where everything is said to be permitted and within reach. To act is in a strict sense a quality of the concrete individual, and it is measured on the outside, just as exposed to the scrutiny of others as one's own gaze.

Against this background, depression is the form illness assumes in the era of self-determination and practical autonomy. Sartre's once so bold thesis – that you are condemned to freedom and that you 'are' your act, that your act defines you at any time, and that thinking otherwise is a proof of 'bad faith' – has become true of society in an age of individualization. The ideal of authenticity – admittedly in an aestheticized version rather than an ethical one, and interpreted in a constructivist manner in the form of so-called continuous *staging* – has lost its critical historical sting and has long since been taken over by advertising as the language everyone speaks; there will soon not be a product that is too trivial to symbolize the 'choice of identity' of the consumer, signalling who he or she wishes to be. The ideal of the uniqueness and authenticity of the individual has in no time at all made a brilliant career for itself as the lubricant of consumerism. While Sartre's militant, atheistic existentialism, with its mocking of the formative power of tradition, convention and the classes (especially the hated bourgeoisie) over the individual's self-understanding and choice of action created a furore in the 1940s and '50s, such individualism is now the opposite of a philosophical provocation: it has been caught up by the age and has merged with it. What would be provocative nowadays is the diametrically opposite move to the early Sartre's: to play the collective against the individual, to give community, tradition and experience priority over individuality, fixation on the moment and on gaining instant gratification for all sorts of perceived needs.

To sum up: as long as the question was 'Am I allowed to do this?', the individual could to a certain extent blame society if he went beyond what was permitted. Society set the limits for the individual's actions. In Freud's classic neurosis there was thus an element of outward aggression, of the individual's opposition to what society had established. Though a social critic in his own right, Freud also believed that this tension between the drives of the individual and the norms of society in many instances would prove productive, enabling – by way of sublimation – the overcoming of primitive narcissism and the creation of great works of art and science. However, as soon as the question changes to 'Am I able to do this?', the aggression that arises in the wake of doing wrong – now synonymous with choosing wrong, i.e. non-optimally – is turned inward rather than outward. This is perfectly in accordance with psychology's original definition of depression: depression is auto-aggression, the attack of the individual on himself. Today, this means that depression intensifies the paralysis of action that helped produce it in the first place.

The idea that the individual lives his life in an ongoing process of self-creation, that we are *entrepreneurs* should, in my opinion, be recognized for what it is and what it indeed functions as: namely, an ideological conception in the nearly forgotten Marxist sense of the word. That it is far removed from expressing the truth about human existence is something I have tried to indicate by drawing attention to what I call the invariable fundamental conditions of life: dependency, vulnerability, mortality, the precariousness of interpersonal relations and existential loneliness. It is not individuals spontaneously and separately but the culture of which they – we – are members that forms the individuals' perception of these fundamental conditions, of whether they are acknowledged or denied, assessed as being meaningful or something entirely negative that has to be fought against or manipulated or controlled by shifting their reality over onto certain others so that one can hope to avoid the discomfort they give rise to. In social reality what is experienced and so acted upon as true is more important that what may be held to be philosophically true. The idea of the individual always and without exception only having to thank himself, only having his own 'choices' to refer to in order to explain why things turned out as they did, assumes a certain sociological validity to the degree that more and more people actually believe it, interpret others and themselves with the aid of it, and act accordingly. This notion has been encouraged by the most widespread and discussed sociological diagnoses of our present time. Such writers as Anthony Giddens and Ulrich Beck have not been clear enough in their criticism of the voluntarism, of the illusion of the almost total freedom of the individual to create (construct) and recreate himself that so obviously fits like a glove the view of the market as the arena of freedom (i.e. of all choices) in particular and with the entrepreneurial view of humanity in general. Seen from the point of view of this ideology the young people of today are to be considered 'life project constructors' obliged to keep all their options open as long as possible and constantly maintain the ability and willingness to re-choose. Whatever you do, whatever you attempt, do not let anything stick to you. Never rest on your laurels. Do not take anything for granted. Remember that the only sure thing is that everything is in a state of flux, that everything you have gathered in the form of knowledge, experience and competence can tomorrow be said to be outdated (or to have exceeded its shelf life). Always remember you have to sell yourself to survive. Work on the ongoing perfection of the commodity that you are.

Richard Sennett talks about the 'corrosion of character'.[52] The corrosion must be seen in connection with the exhaustion that results from the individual constantly having to consider and restlessly assess and re-assess his choices (those taken and those to come) and to update his mental capacities. The demands of the workplace as regards flexibility, mobility and ability to adapt lead to disorientation and gradually to a meltdown or dissolving of the personality, of the intactness and vitality of the self, if we are to believe Sennett's empirically based analysis. In a society where work continues to maintain its position as a key element in the individual's sense of self-worth, increased competition and the compulsion to be flexible lead to a permanent fear of losing one's job, of being weighed and found wanting, at any time at all. The individual is taking part in an uninterrupted exam; he ends up constantly chasing his own rentability and his ability to sell himself, not only to a potential employer but also as a general asset. Attractiveness, understood as present market value, has become the standard of evaluation that all arenas have in common, no matter how dissimilar they otherwise are. As a consequence of his fear of falling short, of falling through or landing up on the outside of society and becoming ostracized, the individual must always be at top-performance level, even though he does not have the necessary time to concentrate. And to the extent a space for stillness and contemplation should happen to arise, the individual starts wondering what can be *done* with it – apart from instrumentalizing it in the form of 'recharging the batteries'. Did someone say quality time? Ask the youngsters. Quality time is when dad is out with the kids and still has his cell phone on, since switching it off – even in the evening and at the weekends – is regarded as taking time out and thus committing the mortal sin of not being accessible. The dream of consumerism, to create a situation of instant gratification of all one's wishes, catches up with and engulfs individuals in the selfsame dynamics – in the form of the unlimited accessibility of the individual, exemplified by the entry of email at all workplaces and in all modern homes with career-conscious adults and (especially) by the omnipresence of the cell phone. Where are the free spaces where the pressure to perform and the anxiety it produces are conspicuous by their absence? Where – to shift the emphasis slightly – are the possibilities of developing a freedom *from* the role of consumer and customer?

There are many reasons for such free spaces becoming fewer. For a start, consider the changed role of medicine. In modern Western society, people do not expect to find the meaning of life by turning towards an inherent cosmic order (the thinking of antiquity), towards an all-powerful God, or towards moral authorities in society. Instead, they expect to find it by turning inwards. As I touched on earlier, *authenticity* – the ideal with roots in Romanticism of being in contact with one's innermost feelings, wishes and aspirations, understood as marking one's uniqueness – has attained a key position in recent times. The language of authenticity has become a natural way of describing all this inner world that the individual carries around with him. What is relatively new, however, is how medicine in general and doctors in particular now participate in the efforts to realize the wish for self-change. Over the last couple of decades doctors have begun to offer physical treatment to alleviate psychological and social problems. Synthetic growth hormones are given to boys to help them avoid the stigma of being short; Propecia is given to middle-aged men to help them avoid the stigma of being prematurely bald; shyness has recently become diagnosed as a distinct psychopathology – one can only wonder what's next . . . Gradually, as the increase of psychological wellbeing is regarded as a legitimate aim for modern medicine, there has been a tremendous rise in the medical states that can apparently be treated.

Again, I am not denying that this development has many good sides to it. Nevertheless, in the context of our discussion here we need to ask a question concerning what I shall call 'cultural complexity'. While on the one hand we find it difficult to condemn individuals (often people we know) who, for example, use plastic surgery to transform themselves in accordance with prevailing aesthetic standards, it must on the other hand be admitted that these 'aids' contribute at a *social* level to consolidating and strengthening the problems it set out to solve. The more people in East Asia use cosmetic surgery to make their eyes look more European, the stronger the social norm becomes that says that East Asian eyes are something one ought to be ashamed of and therefore something the individual must be responsible for doing something about, insofar as such transformation has now become possible: there's a market out there offering remedies and promising improvement. The list of examples of the same phenomenon is long: just think of pale skin, large breasts, 'Jewish' noses and big butts. There is no end to the list.

The pressure from the market, from leading commercial companies, intensifies the trend. Anti-depressants have been the most profitable type of pills in the United States for several years now. The troubling fact, however, is that anti-depressants are not only used to treat serious clinical depression. To an increasing extent, they are used to treat various forms of social anxiety, post-traumatic stress symptoms, various forms of compulsive behaviour, eating disorders, sexual obsessions and compulsions, premenstrual dysphoric troubles, etc. Once again, the list is continually being added to, without stopping at any natural and necessary final point. Several of the disorders I have listed were considered either rare or non-existent until recently. But as soon as a pharmaceutical company develops a treatment for a psychological disorder, it has a vested economic interest in ensuring that doctors make the diagnosis in question as often as possible. The more people who become convinced that they have a disorder and who are persuaded by experts and advertising that it can be treated, the more medicines the company will be able to sell. And, as we have seen, the more customers, the stronger the social pressure on those with the disorders in question who have yet to visit the market and make use of what is on offer. When cosmetic surgery is becoming more and more normalized, this just raises the bar, so that what looks beautiful today will look less beautiful tomorrow. The huge fashion industry, by creating iconic figures – celebrities – of worldwide fame and reach, insists that it promotes individuality and variation. But the effect is the opposite: it is to suck out variety and to undermine the confidence of the large majority of not-so-famous people that their – meaning *my* – looks, and so my difference from those deemed iconic models of beauty, are perfectly OK as they are, and so in no need whatsoever of makeover and 'improvement'.

This being so, what is worth criticizing about this mixing of psychology, medicine and commerce is the lucrativeness of putting pressure on people's self-esteem and constantly reminding them of 'faults' that can be removed or relieved. Generally speaking, the consumerism driven by present-day global capitalism thrives on making us detest our bodies and being dissatisfied with our looks. Anxious and needy, we are better customers. To be comfortable with and so ready to rest content with the way we are and the way we look, would indeed be disastrous for capitalism in general and the self-help industries in particular. Even more important to my main argument is another aspect, however. What does the development in question tell us about pain, about the view of pain and about tolerance regarding what I call invariable fundamental conditions?

I cannot help but see the advance of medicinal technologies – self-modification technologies – and their status as 'the solution' to 'problems' as a new stage in our culture's yearning for mastery. The technologies reflect a sensibility where the world is seen as something to be manipulated and controlled. Positive eugenics (i.e., that parents shall have the right to determine their children's genetic profile, so as to optimize their preferences) can be seen as a sign that as a culture we are in the process of 'playing God'.[53] I am concerned about this sensibility's lack of humility: the arrogance of having such a boundless belief in man-made technology being able to 'solve' all 'problems' connected to our imperfection in both a physical and a (wide and increasingly over-stretched) psychological sense. The step from declaring that something ought not to be to attempting to make sure in the future that it will not be is also short. Here I am not just thinking of all sorts of psychological afflictions (what used to be referred to as 'complexes') but also of fundamental aspects of what it means to be a human being; aspects which until recently have been viewed as unchangeable, such as ageing and, ultimately, death. The presumption I am referring to consists in changing, redefining and transforming what initially was non-optional, and as such given unrequested, to something optional, something that is an object of choice, of forming, of a repertoire of alternatives, made accessible by new technological discoveries. A twofold promise is being made: on the one hand, enhanced self-confidence and sellability; on the other, the reduction or, ultimately, end of pain in one's life. Both promises are presented as within reach in the form of so many incessantly 'improved' products in an ever-expanding 'lifestyle' and 'quality of life' market – a market targeting the most well-off segments, to be sure, yet effecting a change in how people in general tend to look on such a phenomenon as ageing. Across socioeconomic and class-based divisions, pressure is growing to make use of and so profit from the methods now emerging to fix or preempt whatever imperfections one becomes aware of. The hubris at work in this whole development consists in individualizing the transformation of the non-choosable to the choosable, i.e. placing the responsibility for a successful development of the possibility of making choices on the shoulders of the single individual, 'liberated' as he is said to be from collective bonds as well as supernatural authorities of every kind.

My normative assertion is that the limitless freedom to choose, to choose between an ever-increasing number of alternatives in an ever-increasing number of areas of life, is actually for very many people the exact opposite, i.e. an increased – and ever-increasing – coercion of choice. Furthermore, by this coercion being linked to every single individual, as the very proof of that individual's ability to take 'responsibility' in the form of demonstrated self-modification and self-improvement, the pressure increases to choose correctly, to always use one's energies in an optimal way, to a point where this takes the form of self-exhaustion, apathy and depression. The result of contemporary culture's formidable efforts to master pain in existence, namely by trying to outwit all the sources of pain within man as well as the outside symptoms, seems to be that life becomes more painful, not in a physical sense, but in the sense of psychic stress. When everything that exists is open to intervention for the sake of so-called improvement, when nothing can be allowed to remain as it is, when every achieved change has to be replaced by and outdone by new and yet newer ones, when the psyche – the identity, self-esteem – is included in the all-encompassing imperative of self-modification just as much as are our physical natures, it is high time to ask the question of what – and whom – this tyranny in the name of freedom and individuality is *really* benefiting.

Conclusion

In what was to be her last book, *Regarding the Pain of Others*, Susan Sontag contrasts the religious and secular views of pain. In an understanding rooted in religious conceptions, it is possible to see pain – even extreme pain, even that of a child – as something *more* than pain by linking human suffering to sacrifice and renunciation, and thus to exaltation, the gaining of a higher spiritual level, beyond the frailty and (apparent) meaninglessness of earthly life. For the modern sensibility, on the other hand, shaped as it is by the loss of religion's authority, in terms of both morals and interpretation, it is impossible to see anything else than sheer negativity in pain, understood as human suffering: 'Suffering is regarded as something that is a mistake or an accident or a crime. Something to be fixed. Something to be refused. Something that makes one feel powerless.'[54] In short, pain in the form of suffering has assumed for us today the form of what absolutely should not exist, what is completely without purpose and justification. A kind of metaphysical fault, in other words – something faulty about the world, perhaps? Or an anthropological fault – something faulty about us humans? Or both?

Suggesting an answer to 'Why pain?' can easily appear like allying oneself with the – highest earthly – powers that actively inflict pain, that assert that the suffering they cause has a purpose, one that justifies it. Let us instead take the question in a different direction.

Elaine Scarry records a shift in society's attitude towards pain from the nineteenth to the twentieth century, a shift that is still getting stronger. She quotes various aphorisms by the most prominent thinkers and writers of the nineteenth century. Karl Marx wrote: 'There is only one antidote to mental suffering, and that is physical pain.' Oscar Wilde: 'God spare me physical pain, and I'll take care of moral pain myself.' And George Eliot lets one of the characters in a novel remark that 'physical pain might lift me out of my self-absorbed boredom long enough to help me avoid damaging myself'.[55] Only a century – the twentieth – that produces previously unattainable material and physical welfare for humanity (more precisely, for the best-situated classes) can develop an endless fascination with the details of psychic pain, discomfort and disorders. Earlier eras were on the other hand familiar with the privileges implicit in psychiatrically diagnosed madness.

Scarry is drawing our attention to something important. She apparently believes that it is the prejudice of our age that psychic pain is more powerful than physical pain, that significance and meaning – so central to twentieth-century philosophy, especially existentialism – are determined by mental rather than physical reality, by a subject-related relationship rather than anything objective; that the physical is psychologically as well as morally inferior, second-rate, measured against the mental.

Is this how it is? Have we who live today forgotten the dominance of physical pain over psychic pain – over all mental (cognitive as well as affective) content whatsoever? Have we forgotten the validity of Scarry's remarks such as: 'Physical pain is able to obliterate psychological pain because it obliterates all psychological content, painful, pleasurable, and neutral. Our recognition of its power to end madness is one of the ways in which, knowingly or unknowingly, we acknowledge its power to bring to end all aspects of self and world.'[56]

What is the message? That the above – dwelling, so typical of the age, on the individual's exhaustion and the mental sufferings that accompany it – is to be thought of as a luxury problem? Does not the fact that psychic pain in our era seem to overshadow physical pain betray the fact that we are in the process of forgetting what *real* pain is? Could the truth be that the obsession with our own welfare, our own success and perfection, both *of* and *in* the purely external, is a sign of – possibly morbid – narcissism? That since the problem of pain is well on the way to being resolved in our society, as that of hunger is, we are investing increasing amounts of energy – including the latest innovations within psychotherapy and biomedical technologies – in the ostensible 'combating' of what objectively seen are ever-diminishing problems, ever more trivial forms of pain, in an age where pain in some strange way has become identical with 'mental' pain, to the almost complete disparagement of physical pain?

Scarry's reminder that physical pain not only subjectively but in an undeniably objective way is to be regarded as the pain *par excellence* given humanity's constitution, is certainly pertinent. As she points out, once intense physical pain first occurs, it removes everything else from our consciousness and bodily sensual perception. It reduces to nothing the self that has a world – and the world only an intact self can have. This reminder is an important corrective to the priority of the mental which is increasingly being taken for granted in our culture-formed perception of pain, and which has – for good or bad – informed my discussion in this book.

As we have seen, pain born of physical wear and tear has diminished in our society at the same time as pain nurtured by psychological stress has dramatically increased. In the above analysis one of the aims was to show that in times of comprehensive societal change violent pressure is exerted on the single individual. In our age the individual is conceived as the instance where everything has both its beginning and its end – as the yardstick of all values. When the individual becomes his own yardstick, when the relation to the self becomes the place where success is to be developed and evaluated, where all required resources and capacities are to be acquired and the batteries recharged, the consequence is that the risk of a solid '*Erschöpfung an sich selbst*' (Hegel) – the exhaustion of the self from itself – is intensified. *This pain* is conspicuous by its absence in Scarry's perspective. Can it compete with physical pain (in Scarry's sense of the term, bound to the body) as the most painful that a human being can experience?

What can be said to be pain's trump card, the pain over all pains, is perhaps not the most important thing. Whether it is physical or mental, or a combination of both, pain is *equiprimordial* with human existence as such, and must always be lived – tolerated – by the single individual; although it is more shareable with others, more accessible for cultural symbolization, than Scarry would have us believe when she allows physical pain to be a paradigm for the phenomenon of pain as such. If we ignore torture and illness/injury, physical pain is the product of necessity, of the wear and tear of the body, its efforts and occasional exhaustion in man's interaction with outside nature. Wear refers to work, to the loads imposed by physical labour. For most of us, *that* pain – born of necessity and compulsion, as opposed to being sought voluntarily – belongs to a bygone age. Our pain – yes, let us say *our*, not even mine or yours, in accordance with the ideologically postulated either/or of individualization, also within the field of pain – is a quite different pain. It is, most simply expressed, the pain of still being vulnerable to the reality of pain, as humanity has always been – with the important historical and cultural difference that everyone today tolerates his own vulnerability just as badly as that of others.

REFERENCES

1 Elaine Scarry, *The Body in Pain: The Making and Unmaking of the World* (Oxford, 1985), p. 57.
2 Ibid.
3 Per Nortvedt, personal communication, 2004.
4 See Stanley Leavy, *The Psychoanalytic Dialogue* (New Haven, CT, 1980), chap. 1.
5 Sigmund Freud, *Beyond the Pleasure Principle* (London, 1984).
6 Jon Morgan Stokkeland, personal communication, 2004.
7 Sigmund Freud, *Mourning and Melancholia* (London, 1984).
8 Jean-Paul Sartre, *Being and Nothingness* (New York, 1956), p. 104.
9 See Jean-Paul Sartre, *Sketch for a Theory of the Emotions* (London, 1971).
10 Finn Nortvedt and Per Nortvedt, *Smerte – fenomen og forståelse* (Oslo, 2001), p. 60. See also Maurice Merlau-Ponty, *The Phenomenology of Perception* (London, 1970).
11 Nortvedt and Nortvedt, *Smerte – fenomen og forståelse*, p. 72.
12 See Martin Heidegger, *Being and Time* (New York, 1962).
13 David Riesman et al., *The Lonely Crowd* (New Haven, CT, 1950).
14 Heidegger, *Being and Time*, pp. 269ff.
15 Alv Dahl and Eva Dalsegg, *Sjarmør og tyrann. Et innsyn i psykopatens og ofrenes verden* (Oslo, 2001), p. 167.
16 Eva Tryti, 'Dagliglivets ondskap', *Samtiden*, IV (2002).
17 Alice Miller, *For Your Own Good* (London, 1987); *The Untouched Key* (London, 1990).
18 See Melanie Klein, *Love, Guilt and Reparation and Other Works, 1921–1945* (London, 1988).
19 See Freud, *On Metapsychology* (London, 1984), pp. 290ff.
20 See Svein Haugsgjerd, *Lidelsens karakter i ny psykiatri* (Oslo,

1990), p. 307.

21 See Klein, *Envy and Gratitude and Other Works, 1946–1963* (London, 1988).

22 Haugsgjerd, *Lidelsens karakter I ny psykiatri*, p. 309.

23 Ibid., p. 314.

24 See Hanna Segal, 'On Symbol Formation', in *The Work of Hanna Segal* (London, 1986).

25 Max Horkheimer and Theodor W. Adorno, *The Dialectic of Enlightenment* (London, 1974).

26 Klein, *Envy and Gratitude*.

27 C. Fred Alford, *What Evil Means to Us* (New Haven, CT, 1997), p. 108.

28 Ibid., p. 102.

29 Ibid., p. 126.

30 See Colin McGinn, *Ethics, Evil, and Fiction* (Oxford, 1999), pp. 70ff.

31 Heinrich Himmler quoted in Gitta Sereny, *The German Trauma* (London, 2000), p. 295.

32 Alford, *What Evil Means to Us*, p. 108.

33 Alford, *The Psychoanalytic Theory of Greek Tragedy* (New Haven, CT, 1992), p. 63.

34 Thomas Ziehe and Herbert Stubenrauch, *Ny ungdom og usædvanlige læreprocesser* (Copenhagen, 1983).

35 Stig Rune Lofnes quoted in *Aftenposten* (9 August 2004). See also Knud E. Løgstrup, *The Ethical Demand* (Pittsburg, 1994).

36 Lill Scherdin, *Kontrollkulturer og etikk satt på spissen* (Oslo, 2003), p. 608.

37 Loic Wacquant quoted in Scherdin, *Kontrollkulturer*, p. 614. See also Pierre Bourdieu et al., *The Weight of the World* (Oxford, 1999).

38 Elliott Curries quoted in Scherdin, *Kontrollkulturer*, p. 614.

39 Regina General, 'Qualen macht spass', *Freitag* (18 June 2004).

40 See Arne Johan Vetlesen and Jan-Olav Henriksen, *Moralens sjanser i markedets tidsalder* (Oslo, 2003), chap. 1.

41 See Pierre Bourdieu, *Distinction* (London, 1984).

42 Roy Andersson, *Vår tids redsel for alvor* (Oslo, 2003), pp. 17f.

43 See Zygmunt Bauman, *Freedom* (London, 1988) and Richard Sennett, *Respect in a World of Inequality* (New York, 2003).

44 Finn Skårderud, 'Tapte ansikter', in *Skam*, ed. Trygve Wyller (Bergen, 2001), p. 49.

45 Ibid.

46 Emile Durkheim, *The Suicide* (London, 1964).

47 C. Fred Alford, *Whistleblowers: Organizational Power and Broken Lives* (Ithaca, NY, 2001).

48 See Zygmunt Bauman, *Globalization: The Human Consequences* (Oxford, 1999); *Liquid Modernity* (Oxford, 2000).

49 See Ulrich Beck, *Risk Society: Towards a New Modernity* (London, 1992).

50 Rasmus Willig, 'Optionssamfundet og dets patologiske udviklingstendenser', (Roskilde, 2002), p. 17.

51 Alain Ehrenberg, 'Die Müdigkeit, man selbst zu sein', in *Endstation. Sehnsucht. Kapitalismus und Depression*, ed. Claudia Hegemann (Berlin, 2000), p. 125.

52 Richard Sennett, *The Corrosion of Character* (New York, 1998).

53 See Jürgen Habermas, *The Future of Human Nature* (Oxford, 2004).

54 Susan Sontag, *Regarding the Pain of Others* (London, 2003), p. 88.

55 Elaine Scarry, *The Body in Pain*, p. 33.

56 Ibid., p. 34.

BIBLIOGRAPHY

Alford, C. Fred, *Melanie Klein and Critical Social Theory* (New Haven, CT, 1989)

—, *The Psychoanalytic Theory of Greek Tragedy* (New Haven, CT, 1992)

—, *What Evil Means to Us* (New Haven, CT, 1997)

—, *Whistleblowers: Broken Lives and Organizational Power* (New Haven, CT, 2002)

Amery, Jean, *Jenseits von Schuld und Sühne* (Munich, 1988)

Andersson, Roy, *Vår tids redsel for alvor* (Oslo, 2003)

Bauman, Zygmunt, *Globaliseringen og dens menneskelige konsekvenser* (Oslo, 1998)

—, *Liquid Modernity* (Oxford, 2000)

Beck, Ulrich, *Risikogesellschaft. Der Weg in eine andere Moderne* (Frankfurt, 1986)

—, *The Brave New World of Work* (Oxford, 2000)

Dahl, Alv and Eva Dalsegg, *Sjarmør og tyrann. Et innsyn i psykopatenes og ofrenes verden* (Oslo, 2001)

Danner, Mark, 'The Logic of Torture', *New York Review of Books* (24 June 2004), pp. 70–74

Durkheim, Emile, *Selvmordet* (Suicide) (Oslo, 1978)

Dyregrov, Atle, 'Voldelige videospill gjør barn aggressive' (Violent video games make children aggressive), *Aftenposten* (10 August 2004), p. 8

Ehrenberg, Alain, 'Die Müdigkeit, man selbst zu sein', in *Endstation. Sehnsucht. Kapitalismus und Depression*, ed. Claudia Hegemann (Berlin, 2000), pp. 103–39

Elliott, Carl, 'For Better or Worse', *Guardian Weekly* (11 June 2004), p. 14

Freud, Sigmund, *On Metapsychology* (Harmondsworth, 1984)

—, *Jenseits des Lustprinzips* (Frankfurt, 1974)

General, Regina, 'Qualen macht spass', *Freitag* (18 June 2004), p. 2

Habermas, Jürgen, *The Future of the Human Race* (Oxford, 2003)

Haugsgjerd, Svein, *Lidelsens karakter i ny psykiatri* (The Nature of Suffering in Modern Psychology) (Oslo, 1990)

Hegemann, Claudia, ed., *Endstation. Sehnsucht. Kapitalismus und Depression* (Berlin, 2000)

Heidegger, Martin, *Sein und Zeit* (Tübingen, 1927)

Honneth, Axel, ed., *Pathologien des Sozialen* (Frankfurt, 1995)

—, *Leiden an Unbestimmtheit. Eine Aktualisierung der Hegelschen Rechtsphilosophie* (Stuttgart)

Horkheimer, Max and Theodor Adorno, *Dialektik der Aufklärung* (Frankfurt, 1969)

Kirkengen, Anne Luise, *Inscribed Bodies* (Dordrecht, 2001)

Klein, Melanie, *Love, Guilt and Reparation and Other Works 1921–1945* (London, 1988)

—, *Envy and Gratitude and Other Works 1946–1963* (London, 1988)

Lasch, Christopher, *The Culture of Narcissism* (New York, 1979)

——, *The Minimal Self: Psychic Survival in Troubled Times* (London, 1984)

Leavy, Stanley, *The Psychoanalytic Dialogue* (New Haven, CT, 1980)

Lingis, Alphonso, *Abuses* (Berkeley, CA, 1994)

—, *The Community of Those Who Have Nothing in Common* (Bloomington, IN, 1994)

Lofnes, Stig Rune, 'Farligere samfunn med dataspill' (More dangerous societies with computer games), *Aftenposten* (9 August 2004), p. 8

Løgstrup, Knud E., *Norm og spontaneitet* (Norm and spontaneity) (Copenhagen, 1974)

McGinn, Colin, *Ethics, Evil, and Fiction* (Oxford, 1999)

Merleau-Ponty, Maurice, *The Phenomenology of Perception* (London, 1964)

Miller, Alice, *Barneskjebner* (Children's life stories) (Oslo, 1980)

Nietzsche, Friedrich, *Genealogie der Moral* (Stuttgart, 1974)

—, *Jenseits von Gut und Böse* (Stuttgart, 1974)

Nortvedt, Finn and Per Nortvedt, *Smerte – fenomen og forståelse* (Pain – phenomenon and understanding) (Oslo, 2001)

Riesman, David, *The Lonely Crowd* (New Haven, CT, 1950)

Rose, Gillian, *Love's Work* (London, 1995)

Sartre, Jean-Paul, *Being and Nothingness* (New York, 1956)

Scarry, Elaine, *The Body in Pain: The Making and Unmaking of the World* (Oxford, 1985)

Scherdin, Lill, 'Kontrollkulturer og etikk satt på spissen' (Control cultures and ethics taken to their logical conclusion), PhD thesis, Institutt for kriminologi og rettssosiologi, University of Oslo (2003)

Sennett, Richard, *The Corrosion of Character: Work in the 'New' Capitalism* (New York, 1998)

Sereny, Gitta, *The German Trauma* (Harmondsworth, 2000)

Skårderud, Finn, 'Tapte ansikter' (Lost faces); 'Det tragiske mennesket' (Tragic man), in *Skam. Perspektiver på skam, ære og skamløshet i det moderne* (Shame: Perspectives on shame, honour and shamelessness in modern society), ed. Trygve Wyller (Bergen, 2001), pp. 37–68

Sontag, Susan, *Regarding the Pain of Others* (London, 2003)

Taylor, Charles, *The Ethics of Authenticity* (Cambridge, 1992)

Tryti, Eva, 'Dagliglivets ondskap' (The evil of everyday life), *Samtiden*, iv (2002), pp. 116–24

Vesaas, Halldis Moren, *Livshus* (Life house) (Oslo, 1995)

Vetlesen, Arne Johan and Per Nortvedt, *Følelser og moral* (Emotions and morals) (Oslo, 1996)

Vetlesen, Arne Johan and Erik Stänicke, *Fra hermeneutikk til psykoanalyse* (From hermeneutics to psychoanalysis) (Oslo, 1999)

Vetlesen, Arne Johan and Jan-Olav Henriksen, *Moralens sjanser i markedets tidsalder* (The chances of ethics in an age of the market) (Oslo, 2003)

Vetlesen, Arne Johan, *Menneskeverd og ondskap. Essays og artikler* (Human value and evil: Essays and articles) *1991–2002* (Oslo, 2003)

Willig, Rasmus, 'Optionssamfundet og dets patologiske udviklingstendenser' (The option society and its pathological tendencies), ms, Roskilde University, Denmark, 2002

Winnicott, Donald, *Playing and Reality* (Harmondsworth, 1980)

Wyller, Trygve, ed., *Skam. Perspektiver på skam, ære og skamløshet i det moderne* (Shame. Perspectives on shame, honour and shamelessness in modern society) (Bergen, 2001)

Yalom, Irvin D., *Existential Psychotherapy* (New York, 1980)

Ziehe, Thomas and Herbert Stubenrauch, *Ny ungdom og usæd-vanlige læreprocesser* (Modern youth and unusual learning processes) (Copenhagen, 1983)